Y OF THE ... ARI

fully tried to find it again. In the exclusive article on this page, Mr. Paton tells you of the hopes and plans of the new expedition.

...ty" was given to the world by an American explorer, G. A. Farini, explorers have unsuccess-

...he
...he
...ese
...the
...ote.
...ost City, he continued south, and reached Ki-Ki in three days, this Ki-Ki being far to the north of the southern Ki-Ki of which Mr. Paver writes."

A magic name

COULD Farini have been as far north as Mr. Ibbetson supposes? Is there any mountain in the south of which no one had then seen or heard? Or is the Afrikaans word "berg" used in the Kalahari to describe even a sand-dune? Could it have been the Aha Mountains after all?

These are the questions to which the Flower Expedition hopes to find a reply. But it should be made quite clear that we are not an expedition of experts.

We are going to give Reg Ibbetson every possible help in the testing of his theory; but we find that easy to do because the Kalahari is for us a magic place with a magic name. For a month we shall be in the desert, and do not expect to see any white man, to read any newspaper, to send or receive any message, or to hear any political speech.

I will wash dishes

MAJOR FLOWER is our leader, but for the sake of mortifying his flesh (and ours), he will also be cook. Reg Ibbetson is our second-in-command, and also the camera man. Raymond White, Len Tree, and Brian Pole are drivers and maintenance men. Keith Walker is our navigator. I myself shall keep a record of the journey, and wash the dishes. But we shall have another record too, in the shape of 5,000 feet of colour film. Who knows? We may be the first to show the Lost City to the world.

Night is bitter

THE expedition will travel on a Diesel truck loaned by a well-known British firm of manufacturers. The truck will carry a jeep and large quantities of fuel and water. The expeditionaries will take a large number of blankets, because the Kalahari night is bitter; a generous allowance of simple and balanced foods; a moderate amount of alcohol; and some goods for gifts and barter.

I myself hope that we shall...

Drawing by Peter Chiswell.

Lost City

...most scientific and ...norough attempt made to ...the Lost City was under-...en by Mr. F. R. Paver, now ...Hi. Crest, Natal.

He ...plored a region far to the ...th of that to be visited by ... Flower Expedition. He ...nsiders that the Flower ...pedition is wasting money and himself. "I am convinced," he says, "that the ruins seen by Farini were built by the same people as built Zimbabwe, and in the course of an east-west migration. It appears improbable that they would leave a fertile and well-watered region and go 350 miles south into one of the most arid parts of the world. I believe that Farini was much further north than he supposed.

"He wrote a detailed account

Lost City of the Kalahari

Alan Paton

Lost City of the Kalahari

Alan Paton

Edited and introduced by Hermann Wittenberg

UNIVERSITY OF KWAZULU-NATAL PRESS

Published in 2005 by University of KwaZulu-Natal Press
Private Bag X01
Scottsville 3209
South Africa
Email: books@ukznpress.ac.za
www.ukznpress.co.za

© Paton text and all APC memorabilia: Anne Paton 2005
© Introduction: Hermann Wittenberg 2005
©Terence Spencer photographs: Gallo Images

ISBN: 1-86914-066-4

All rights reserved. No part of this publication may be reproduced or transmitted in any form or by any means, electronic or mechanical, including photocopying, recording or any information storage and retrieval system, without prior permission in writing from University of KwaZulu-Natal Press.

Editor: Hermann Wittenberg
Layout: Flying Ant Designs
Cover Designer: Sebastien Quevauvilliers
Front Cover Photograph: Baobab Tree by Terence Spencer (courtesy of Gallo Images)
Back Cover Photograph: From the Ibbetson family scrapbook
Frontispiece photograph of Alan Paton by Terence Spencer (courtesy of Gallo Images)

Printed and bound by Interpak Books, Pietermaritzburg

Note: Although contentious, the original term "Bushmen" has been retained in Paton's narrative (and, correspondingly, in the Introduction), since this was the terminology in use during the 1950s. This term has been replaced in some contemporary usage by "San", which is in itself problematic, since it derives from a derogatory Nama word.

The terms "tame" and "wild" Bushmen, though possibly offensive to contemporary readers, have similarly been retained in the interests of contextual accuracy. They were used during the period to differentiate between those Bushmen who were amenable to Western contact and those who shunned it.

The word "Hottentot" has now been replaced in contemporary usage with the less offensive "KhoiKhoi".

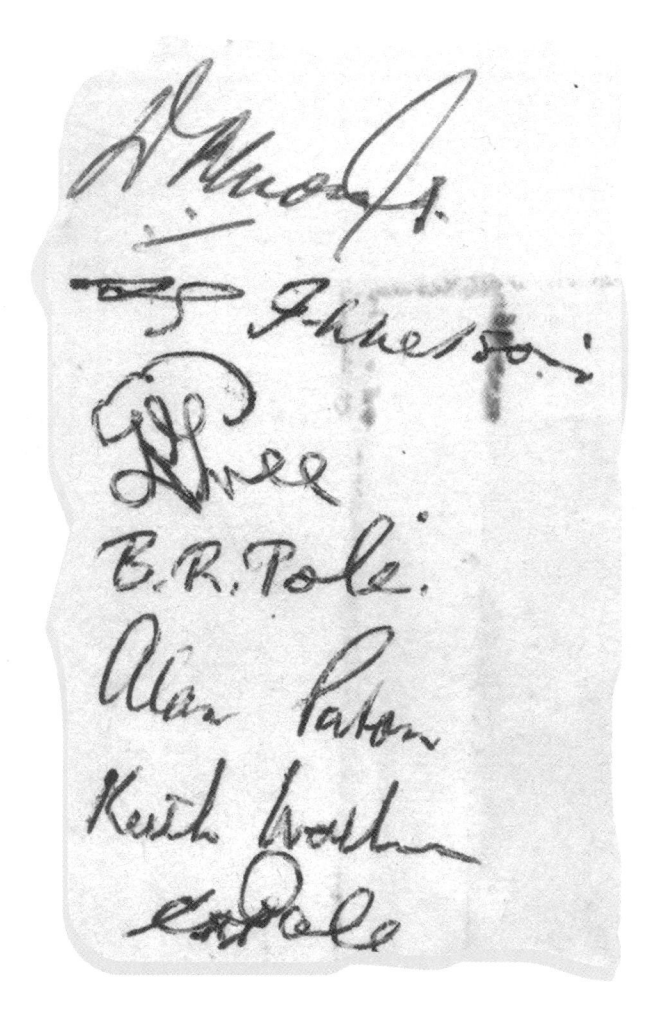

Signatures (from top–bottom): Jock Flower, Sailor Ibbetson, Len Tree, Brian Pole, Alan Paton, Keith Walker and Harold Pole.

Source: Ibbetson family scrapbook (found on a scrap of paper pasted in as a frontispiece)

Contents

Photograph of Zsa Zsa Gabor	viii
Acknowledgements	ix
Extracts of Paton's original diary pages	x
Introduction by Hermann Wittenberg	1
Map showing route through Bechuanaland to Aha Mountains	17
Map from Paton's diary showing route to Kalahari	18
Excerpts from Mission Document of the Natal Kalahari Expedition	20
Telegraph to the *Natal Witness*	23

Lost City of the Kalahari   25

Colour stills from 8 mm film of the Expedition fall between pages 52 and 53

Interview with Brian Pole	53
Biographical Note on Alan Paton	60

Film star Zsa Zsa Gabor holds a copy of the *Natal Witness* (29 May 1956) showing front page article about the Lost City Expedition.

Source: Ibbetson family scrapbook

Acknowledgements

I am grateful to the University of the Western Cape for the research grant that allowed me to travel to Pietermaritzburg in 2003 in order to visit the Alan Paton Centre at the University of KwaZulu-Natal. While looking at Paton's pre-1948 unpublished work, I came across an enigmatically titled folder named "Natal Kalahari Expedition". Among the collection of equipment lists, maps, mileage tallies and other travel-related miscellanea, was a sheaf of pages torn out of a school exercise book that contained Paton's Lost City narrative. I am very grateful for the kind hospitality and assistance of Jewel Koopman and Estelle Liebenberg-Barkhuizen of the Alan Paton Centre, who shared my excitement at the discovery of this remarkable text, and also arranged for the transcription of the original longhand manuscript.

Special thanks are also due to the following people:

Anne Paton, for giving her permission for the publication of this text.

The Ibbetson family, particularly Mr Kevin Ibbetson, for giving his time to answer my many questions about his father, and above all for generously making available the scrapbook of his mother, Jean Ibbetson. It contained numerous newspaper clippings, photographs, letters and other memorabilia relating to the expedition. One of the most significant items in the scrapbook was the only known copy of the typed shorter version of the Lost City narrative.

Brian Pole, for generously giving his time to be interviewed, and also for making available the valuable 8mm film that his father, Harold, took of the expedition (from which the colour stills between pages 52 and 53 are taken).

Julianne Pole, Brian's wife, for her hospitality and invaluable help in tracking down important material relating to the expedition, as well as assisting with copying documents.

Mark Pole, Harold's grandson, for making the fascinating audio tape of his interview with Alan Paton available.

Edwin Wilmsen, for reading the manuscript with interest and verifying the accuracy of Paton's maps.

Colin Gardiner and *Peter Brown*, for answering my queries about the expedition and for providing insight into Paton's life at the time he wrote the Lost City manuscript.

My colleagues at the University of the Western Cape and elsewhere who commented on my research that I presented in the form of two seminars and a conference paper.

Lastly, and most importantly, *Elana Bregin*, of UKZN Press, without whose patient and sure handling of the material and my ideas, this publication would not have been possible.

(1)

I picked up ~~this young man~~ Sailor
Ibbetson ~~just as~~ on the ~~was leaving the city~~ main road from
~~of~~ Pietermaritzburg ~~on my way to~~ to Kloof ~~my home~~
~~at Kloof.~~ He was a nice-looking young fellow with
clean blue eyes, ruddy face, & a powerful body,
though he was a little above medium height. I do
not know how he came to mention the
Kalahari, but ~~the moment~~ he did ~~so~~ it
was clear at once, that he was a fanatic.

"It's the dream of my life to go there,"
he said, "and to find Farini's lost city."

~~This was~~ "Farini?" I said. "Who's Farini?"

In 1884 Mr. G. A. Farini, an
American cattle-rancher, was visiting Coney
Island when he made the acquaintance
of Gert, a half-breed hunter from South
Africa. Gert ~~who~~ had gone to New York as
interpreter for a party of "Earthmen", small
people from the Kalahari.

Gert's account of the Kalahari,
its grass-covered plains, its teeming game, and

to diamonds, determined Farini to visit this paradise that he had always thought to be a desert. He spent several months there with his son Lulu, observing people, plants, & animals, and making notes for his very readable book "Through the Kalahari Desert."

Near the end of his journey he camped beside "a long line of stone which looked like the Chinese Wall after an earthquake." But it turned out to be a man-made wall, built out of worked stones. Farini & his son spent two days there, excavating pavements, & convincing themselves that there indeed had once been "a city, or a place of worship, or the burial-ground of a great nation, perhaps thousands of years ago."

"Haven't other people tried to find this lost city?" I said.

"They went to the wrong place," said Sailor. "They looked too far to the south."

Introduction

Alan Paton's Lost City narrative, published here for the first time, is an important text by the celebrated author of *Cry, the Beloved Country* that has, incredibly, remained virtually unknown until now.[1] It is the only travel writing that we know of in Paton's *oeuvre*, and may well rank as one of the minor classics in South African travel literature.

The Lost City narrative tells the curious story of the Natal Kalahari Expedition that set out in 1956 to find a mythical Lost City in a remote range of mountains deep in the Kalahari Desert of present-day Botswana. Paton's travelogue is an intriguing and compelling mix of superb landscape description, ironic observation and, in some respects, troubling ethnographic exposition, and provides fascinating insight into a private and little-known side of Paton. The Kalahari episode shows Paton in the unfamiliar role of fortune-seeking adventurer, revelling in the camaraderie around campfires and enjoying the "rough company" of other men in the bush. A disarmingly human side of Paton emerges that has been largely obscured by his public stature as a prominent voice of liberal-Christian conscience in South Africa. The picture we have of Paton today is primarily shaped by the enduring success of his famous novel and by his political stance, in particular his moral vision of a society based on values of forgiveness, reconciliation and social justice. In the Kalahari narrative, however, we are given the rare opportunity to encounter Paton less formally – not as a leading intellectual and champion of liberalism, but simply an ordinary man amongst other men, growing an unkempt beard, enthralled by the vast desert landscape, hunting game, roughing it in the bush, and remaining unwashed for weeks.

What makes the Kalahari episode particularly intriguing is the fact that Paton, as far as can be ascertained, subsequently made no public references to it, and omitted any mention of the expedition in his otherwise candid autobiography.[2] Equally puzzling is the fact that the travelogue, a fluent and evocative piece of writing, remained unpublished in his lifetime. This publication of the Lost City narrative, a work very different to any of his other writing, therefore not only makes a previously unknown Paton text available to a wider public, but also contributes towards a fuller understanding of one of South Africa's most celebrated writers.

Setting out on 26 June 1956, Paton, together with six other amateur adventurers from the Natal Midlands, embarked on the grandly titled "Natal Kalahari Expedition" in search of the ruins of a lost, ancient Mediterranean civilisation. They travelled in an old five-ton Austin truck, nicknamed "Kalahari Polka".[3] Despite the fact that its "engine boiled continuously"[4] and that it frequently broke down, the expeditionaries managed to cover almost 3 000 miles in the troublesome vehicle, mostly on bad roads and vague, sandy tracks. The expedition was led by a Nottingham Road farmer (and East Africa Campaign veteran), Major D.C. (Jock) Flower, but its main driving force was Reg (Sailor) Ibbetson, a Hammersdale farmer with a penchant for adventurous get-rich-quick schemes, who was obsessed with G.A. Farini's curious 1886 book, *Through the Kalahari Desert*.[5] Ibbetson was determined to find the ruins of the "Lost City" that Farini, an American showman and cattle-rancher, had allegedly seen. Ibbetson's nick-name, "Sailor", derived not only from his capacity for hard drinking, but also from his war-time service on the HMS Dorsetshire where, according to his son Kevin, he was wounded in the naval battle that led to the sinking of the Bismarck.[6] The other founding members of the party were Keith Walker, a Michaelhouse College Physics teacher, who was to act as the navigator; and Len Tree and Brian Pole, garage hands, who came along as drivers and mechanics. The sixth intended member, Raymond White, dropped out before departure, disillusioned by Ibbetson's unreliability. He was replaced by Brian Pole's father, Harold, with whom Paton appears to have formed a good relationship. The two of them were known respectively as "Pops" and "Uncle" by the rest of the party. Paton's duties were set down as "Scribe and Bottlewasher", according to a logistics and equipment list that was found, posthumously, in Paton's copy of *Roberts' Birds of South Africa* (see p. 20). The document sets out the objective of the expedition ("To find Lost City, by truck and foot patrols"), followed by the conspiratorial injunction that everything had "to be kept secret" – though Ibbetson appears to have outlined his grandiose plans to any journalist who cared to listen. Among the equipment and provisions taken along were items such as sleeping bags, haversacks and great coats, two cases of brandy and copious amounts of food. Besides the provisions of army biscuits and milk powder, there were "200 lbs of mealie meal", presumably to feed local guides and porters and, seeing that this was a Natal expedition, there was also curry powder. The list ends with a curious item: "Knives and Mirrors for Natives", indicating that the expeditionaries expected to barter cheap trinkets while making their way through the desert.

The Kalahari documents are part of Paton's voluminous literary legacy that his widow, Anne Paton, generously donated to the University of Natal, Pietermaritzburg in 1989. They are now preserved in the archives of the Alan Paton Centre. Besides the already referred to list of equipment and provisions, the papers comprise a rough diary whose tattered pages and often jumpy handwriting suggest that it was partly written on the moving truck; two hand-drawn maps of the route; a detailed account of the daily and cumulative mileage;

and a second, incomplete diary written by someone in the party other than Paton (a process of elimination suggests Walker). There are also some miscellaneous items of correspondence, including the copy of a short telegraph which Paton sent to the *Natal Witness* on the 5th July 1956 from Ghanzi:

> truck brought down heavy branch of camelthorn which smashed canopy and came to rest inches from heads of keith walker and self party well cheerful very dirty paton. (see p. 23)

But the most important text in the papers is a 53-page manuscript in Paton's handwriting that provides us with an intriguing account of the month-long journey. This travel narrative contains evocative descriptions of the vast desert and bush landscape, and detailed observations of the people of the Kalahari. With wry, self-deprecating humour the text relates the ardours of travel and the series of misfortunes that befell the party. Undated and untitled, this narrative was evidently written soon after Paton's return.[7] The text published in this book is largely based on this manuscript, though it also incorporates some minor revisions, derived from an abridged typescript version of the original text that was subsequently found in the possession of the Ibbetson family in Pietermaritzburg. This latter version gives us the title, "Lost City of the Kalahari", which had been missing from the original. The reduced length and numerous amendments suggest that Paton perhaps planned to submit it as a magazine article. *Life* magazine was possibly the intended publication, since it had despatched one of its photographers, Terence Spencer, to accompany the expedition. Spencer joined the expedition en route to the Kalahari in the Free State, boarding the truck with two cameras and a case of whiskey. Although Spencer took several hundred images during the trip (some of which are published for the first time in this volume), *Life* subsequently did not go ahead with the Kalahari feature. In the absence of any records, both on the side of Paton and *Life*, we may speculate that the story was shelved due to the failure of the expedition to find any archaeological evidence of the Lost City. As far as can be ascertained, only one of Spencer's pictures (see p. 40) made it into print. This was featured in *Time* magazine accompanying a book review of Paton's 1961 short story collection, *Tales from a Troubled Land*.[8] Spencer later went on to become a famous rock celebrity and showbiz photographer, making his name through his early coverage of the Beatles. Both Ibbetson and Harold Pole took film footage of the expedition, and Pole's material has been generously made available for use in this publication by his son, Brian Pole. It is a 23-minute-long colour film – possibly the earliest film footage of Paton in existence – and records the author and his fellow expeditionaries driving in their psychedelic (and frequently collapsed) truck through the Kalahari bush, and engaging in the day-to-day scenes and experiences of their adventure.

Aside from Paton's Kalahari papers and the other personal records, there was also extensive press coverage of the expedition at the time, as several articles in the *Natal Witness*, *Natal Mercury*, *Natal Daily News*, *Sunday Express* and *The Argus* attest. These reports give a good indication of the extent of Ibbetson's grandiose schemes, and the way in which they sometimes bordered on the fantastic. The *Natal Witness*, for instance, reported on its front page that the "all-Natal expedition" hoped "to make archaeological history", and that "the 22ft diesel truck ... will be fitted with a grapnel to enable it to pull itself out of the deep sand".[9] Ibbetson told journalists that the huge truck was to have two decks, the lower one carrying a jeep, useful for reconnoitring, and that "while separated, the jeep and truck will be in communication by walkie talkie".[10] Even more ambitious plans were fed to *The Argus*, which duly reported that a small aircraft was to accompany the ground crew and assist in making a major archaeological discovery.[11]

One of the tantalising questions raised by the odd expedition is the following: what was the eminently pragmatic and level-headed 53-year-old Paton doing embarking on a colonial-style "African adventure", spending almost a month on the back of a decrepit and excruciatingly uncomfortable truck travelling through the Kalahari wastes with men he hardly knew and with whom he had little in common? The backdrop events of 1956 may provide some clues. This was a particularly demanding period for Paton in his political career. A few months before he embarked on his great Kalahari escapade he had been elected chairman of the non-racial Liberal Party of South Africa. The year before, 1955, had heralded the bitterly contested destruction of Sophiatown, which the liberal circles in which the Patons moved had played a major, but ultimately powerless, role in resisting. Later that year, there was another watershed event which drew the battle lines between the state and progressive forces: the Kliptown People's Congress that adopted the Freedom Charter, subsequently followed by the first Treason Trial. It was a tense period in South Africa, with a rigid and powerful state rolling out the programme of grand apartheid without regard for domestic and international protests. Paton became increasingly drawn into adopting a more active political role in mobilising protest against discriminatory laws, culminating in his brief arrest in December 1956. In his second autobiography, *Journey Continued*, Paton writes that "the year 1956 was a notable year in the life of the Liberal Party" and that he spent many of his weekends "away from home, travelling to almost every town in Natal, and to many in the Transvaal, to speak at large protest meetings".[12]

These events offer an interesting contrasting context from which to view the seemingly impulsive adventure, which Paton in his manuscript terms "the craziest expedition ever to have gone into the unknown". It seems safe to speculate that part of the allure of the expedition for Paton was its very inconsequentiality – the prospect of escape it offered from the intense work demands and increasingly depressing political scenario in which he was embroiled. In the *Sunday Express*, he wrote with relish of the fact that the explorers "shall be in the desert and do not expect to see any white man, to read any newspaper, to send or receive any message, or to hear any political speech".[13] In the light of Paton's progressive political stance and his energetic contributions to the anti-apartheid struggle, the Kalahari Expedition appears less of a colonial anachronism than a fantastic attempt to escape, if only momentarily, from the troubling racial trauma of his country.

But perhaps there is an even simpler answer to the question of why so reputable a figure as Paton should join a quixotic quest for a lost city. One has to look no further than the person of Ibbetson himself. Selwyn George Reginald Ibbetson, to give him his full name, was a charismatic charmer with a gifted tongue. His son Kevin says of his father that "he could hold a room spellbound with stories".[14] While it seems unlikely that Paton, normally a sceptical and cautious man, would have been easily seduced by dubious promises of famous discovery, the storyteller in him would have been highly susceptible to the suggestive force of Ibbetson's personality. This is implied in his own whimsical admission that "Sailor, that Ancient Mariner, had fixed me with his eye". While it is not hard to understand how Paton could have fallen under the mesmeric spell of Ibbetson's beguiling story and the mysterious aura that he wove around the Kalahari and Farini's book, he seems early on in their acquaintance to have got Ibbetson's measure: "It was clear at once that he was a fanatic," he says at the start of the travelogue.

Ibbetson appears to have been a colourful, larger-than-life figure who spent much of his life pursuing fantastic get-rich-quick schemes. He was, by all accounts, a noted womaniser who left a trail of broken hearts and bad debts behind him. He dabbled in illicit diamond buying and had a propensity for being on the move, constantly changing occupations and seldom staying rooted for long before moving his trailer-home to a new town. Nonetheless, he was not only possessed by the vision of a desert treasure, but was also a highly persuasive and charming speaker who could, as Brian Pole remembers, smooth-talk his way out of trouble with ease.[15] The expedition was his brain-child and it was entirely his drive and vision that brought it to fruition. As Paton tells it, Ibbetson originally claimed to have a brand new seven-ton Leyland Albion truck "in the bag", supposedly pressed on him by "a British firm anxious to advertise their product". On setting out, however, he could only produce a second-hand fivetonner, which was, as Brian Pole recalls, in a shocking mechanical condition (see p. 53).[16] Already on the day of departure there was "dismay at the amount of oil used" and on the following day, three miles out of Winburg, there was "a horrible noise in the engine" which necessitated its complete removal in order to replace a broken crankshaft.[17] Mechanical failures continued to hamper the expedition's progress and the improvisational skill and ingenuity of the small-town mechanics from the Natal Midlands – not to mention the provisions of whiskey – proved invaluable to keep up morale. It is a major credit to Ibbetson's leadership that despite the constant mechanical failures and intermittent breakdowns they reached their goal.

After the Kalahari trip, Ibbetson was briefly involved in an abortive attempt to recover gold bullion from the wreck of the *Grosvenor* on the Wild Coast.[18] He then became a minor celebrity when a British film company bought the film rights to a novel he had written about the Kalahari, from which, according to *The Star* he hoped to net R30 000.[19] Ibbetson's book, *Kalahari Fever*, told the story of two friends who had found a diamond treasure in the desert but subsequently became bitter rivals. Zsa Zsa Gabor, who was to play the female lead role, flew down to South Africa to meet Ibbetson. There is a photograph of her, holding the 29 May 1956 edition of the *Natal Witness*, the front page of which carries a report of the Natal Kalahari Expedition (see p. viii). According to Kevin Ibbetson, Gabor and his father supposedly had a brief affair – but whether this was fact or a figment of Ibbetson's fantasy is open to speculation. Nothing ultimately came of the film, and Ibbetson's manuscript has not survived. It was never published and the only copy is now lost.

While Paton's treatment of Ibbetson in the Lost City narrative is largely indulgent and good-humoured, if more than a little tongue-in-cheek, their relationship deteriorated markedly after Paton had penned the piece. It is tempting to speculate that part of the reason for Paton's reluctance to speak about the Kalahari trip after 1956 and to push for publication of the story was because of his disillusionment over the whole affair, due not so much to its lack of tangible outcome, as the bad taste left by being swindled out of a substantial sum of money by Ibbetson. This emerges in an extraordinary interview that was conducted with Paton early in 1988, a few weeks before his death. In this, one of the last interviews of his life, Paton finally talked about the Kalahari Expedition about which he had remained silent for more than 30 years. A tape recording of the interview was tracked down in Pietermaritzburg last year during the course of the research for this book. It was made by Mark Pole, grandson of Harold Pole who, as previously mentioned, had made an 8 mm film of the journey. His grandson thought it an interesting idea to show the old footage to

Paton. Mark's tape recorder was running throughout the screening, but the sound quality is very poor due to the noise of the film projector and it drowns out most of Paton's comments during the viewing. After the film had stopped, however, and the projector was switched off, Paton made a few clearly audible remarks about the events. He described Ibbetson as "a very conceited young man" who "decided he could find the Lost City" despite the fact that "none of us knew anything about archaeology. The only one I believe who might have was the chap from Michaelhouse, I've forgotten his name" (His reference is to Keith Walker). Although Paton's memory had let him down on some details, he had vivid recollections of being cheated out of money by Ibbetson. On the tape, a clearly riled Paton recalls the events in which Ibbetson conned him:

> Ibbetson did not tell me that the truck had been hired from some chap in Durban. Altogether we spent three weeks there and all we found was a stone wall and you'd have to have a very strong imagination to take that for the Lost City. When we came back, one day Ibbetson came to see me at Kloof in a terrible state and said that he was in very great trouble.
> I said, 'Why?'
> 'Because the chap with the truck he never told me that I owed him £400 for the truck. And he said he will take my farm away.'
> So I fished out £400. So in the end I paid for the damn expedition. The others put up seven times £140 and I put up £400 and then Ibbetson gave me the film,[20] sort of as a return. Well, he rang up, 'Can I lend the film?', because some American wanted to see it.
> I said, 'Alright, you can borrow the film', but I never saw it again. It's typical Ibbetson. (Mark Pole Interview, 1988)

Paton's last words about the trip are, however, more positive. He notes that although "as a scientific expedition it was absolutely worthless", as a holiday in the Kalahari it was "good, very good. I enjoyed it".[21]

It is hard to say to what extent Paton felt disillusioned by the failed outcome of the expedition, or whether he ever took its objectives seriously. "I don't care about the Lost City," he writes dismissively in his narrative, "I want to see the Kalahari and the Aha Mountains." Yet the romantic in him may well have hoped for a different outcome. In his meticulous way, he had clearly researched the topic thoroughly. He had read Farini's book with great interest, calling it "very readable", and his comments in the *Sunday Express* article show him to be intrigued by the archaeological mystery and hopeful of a discovery. He even made a special trip to Johannesburg to "gather last-minute information about the 'lost city'", according to a report in the *Natal Daily News*.[22] As part of this research, Paton interviewed a policeman who had once been stationed in a remote Kalahari outpost and supposedly "knew" the location of the ruins.

As bizarre as such a quest might seem from contemporary perspectives, the belief in a lost city of the desert was a widely held obsession in Paton's day. Such myths were tied up with conservative colonial discourses that disparaged any possibility of African cultural or scientific achievement. An example was the popular belief around the ruins of Great Zimbabwe, which disputed the indigenous, African provenance of the elaborate, finely-worked stone structures and attributed their origin to more exotic sources. Ibbetson, like many others, held the belief that "Semitic people worked their way across Africa establishing a chain of forts of which Zimbabwe was the principal". Farini's Lost City in the Kalahari would have constituted another outpost of this fabled ancient northern race before they "left from the West Coast for South America on rafts".[23] Ibbetson talked about mounting a Kontiki-type expedition across the Atlantic that would "prove" his theory. The myth of classical ruins lost in the desert not only inspired the likes of Ibbetson and his fellow Natal adventurers, but gained a wider currency. It is useful to look more carefully at the full extent of the Lost City mania that gripped sections of South Africa's population.

The popular response to Farini's book shows that until at least the mid-1960s, the Lost City remained a powerful imaginary site that stimulated the dreams and fantasies of countless people in South Africa and abroad. Many were inspired to emulate Farini's example and undertake Lost City journeys of their own. A.J. Clement, a Wits University academic, who himself came under the spell of the mythical ruins, lists 27 fully-equipped expeditions between 1932 and 1965, as well as dozens of individual and small-scale quests.[24] One of the best resourced attempts was the 1951 "Panhart-Capricorn Expedition" led by the French explorer Francois Balsan. It included the well-known paleo-anthropologist Philip Tobias, who became more interested in the Middle Stone Age tools that he found in raised terraces along the Nossob River than in the mission's objectives. Tobias, in any case doubtful of Farini's story, subsequently found natural limestone formations near Ky-Ky along the Nossob River that looked like old walls. That settled the matter for Tobias and his findings were reported in *Die Burger* of 6 September 1951 under the headline: "Kalahari se 'Verlore Stad' is maar net kalkformasies" (The Kalahari's "Lost City" is just limestone formations).[25] Balsan, however, left the Kalahari still convinced that there were at least two "real" lost cities to be found there.

Lawrence Green, a well-known and prolific writer on South African travel lore, joined a University of Cape Town expedition in 1936 to find "a Zimbabwe of the Kalahari".[26] Green was inspired by an article by Dr Meent Borcherts of Upington, who was regarded as an authority on the lore of the Lost City. Borcherts and F.R. Paver, a Johannesburg newspaper editor, had explored the Kalahari in 1933, and Paver subsequently published a series of thrilling articles in *The Star* which excited the popular imagination. Paver's journalism played a major role in elevating Farini out of obscurity, but he also later became the Natal Kalahari Expedition's chief critic, attacking Ibbetson's theories in a number of articles.[27]

Borcherts reportedly told Green that he had it from "impeccable sources" that the Lost City existed, thus corroborating Farini's story. But the names of "the two men who declared they had been to the Lost City" had to be kept secret, "for they are farmers who crossed the Bechuanaland border to poach game".[28] Even more fantastical was the story told to Borcherts by a local police sergeant. While on camel patrol in the desert, he had supposedly come across an old stone quarry with some of the remaining squared stones still on the spot, as well as the remains of an ancient, fourteen-foot-long river boat. Green's book alludes to the possibility of a navigable river that once flowed through the desert from Lake Ngami and on whose banks the Lost City must have flourished.

As with all legends, the lore of the Lost City increasingly nourished more tales, which in turn generated a web of stories in which fiction, fact and hearsay blended into an alluring body of rich myth. Lennox van Onselen, who regarded the ruins as "one of the last real mysteries of Darkest Africa" wrote a curious book, *Trekboer*, in which he recounted several Lost City stories, such as that of a certain Charlie Swart "seeing a fabulous ruin of white stones in 1905", as well as reports of "Hottentots bringing out gold ornaments and diamonds".[29] Like the fabled Kruger millions, the story of Farini's Lost City, liberally interleafed with tales of diamond riches to be found there, attracted eccentric amateur historians, fortune-seekers and adventurers. Two Vanderbijlpark mine workers, D. J. Herholdt and J. Daneel, set off one weekend to the Kalahari in an old car, and were forced to forego sleep in order to complete the journey as quickly as possible so as to get back in time for their Monday shift. Herholdt claimed to have been "within six or seven miles of the heart of the city before circumstances forced them to return".[30] A similar story was told by Michael McDonald, a Johannesburg municipal employee, who claimed in his book, *The Voice of Africa* (1961), to have seen a city "beyond Francistown" that "consists only of ruins of houses of 3000 to 5000 people of ancient Phoenecian, Arab, Ethiopian and Hottentot stock. Their cattle were the predecessors of our present Afrikaander cattle".[31]

The expeditionary fervour reached its climax in the 1950s, when at least ten different attempts were made, according to Fay Goldie, who herself participated in aerial and ground searches in the hope of "spectacular and tantalising discoveries".[32] In 1951, a well-known Cape Town surgeon, Dr F. D. du Toit van Zyl made two separate searches and persuaded the Ministry of Defence to loan him an airforce Dakota plane plus aircrew, thus even drawing government resources into the quest. Van Zyl subsequently wrote a warm letter of encouragement to Ibbetson.[33]

The enthusiasm for and obsession with the quest for the Lost City was spread across a wide spectrum of white South African society, ranging from journalists, academics and doctors to adventurous housewives, boy scouts and mineworkers. Indeed, Lost City fervour became such an entrenched part of the cultural landscape that it even found its way into literary satire. In Herman Charles Bosman's short story, "Lost City", one of his backveld characters complains that "you'd have no quiet in the Kalahari. Or room to move. From Molepole onwards it seems that there's just one expedition on top of another, each one searching for a lost city". Bosman poked fun at the obsessive fanaticism of Farini devotees through the sly, deprecating wit of his familiar Groot Marico characters. Jurie Steyn, Bosman's quintessential bushveld ingénue, wonders at the implausibility that "people would go and build a city, and then just lose it", and speculates that perhaps the Lost City cannot be found because thieving Bushmen have made off with it, "washing hanging on the clothes-lines and all".[34]

It is clear from the above that Paton's Kalahari exploit was not simply an isolated, eccentric act but part of a more general obsession with Farini's story that animated many of his contemporaries. Yet even though it provides the impetus for the journey, it is not the Lost City itself that is the focus of Paton's narrative, but the wider experiences of travel, the hauntingly beautiful landscape, and the people of the desert. Although the text situates itself within the larger conventions of colonial exploration and adventure writing, it is Paton's ironic and self-deprecating humour, and his masterful evocation of the Kalahari landscape that is the real strength of the narrative. There is much enjoyment to be found in Paton's wry asides and in the delight he takes in exposing the absurdities of an expedition that fell so far short of its own grandiose ambitions. Leaving at the intended departure time, "on the minute" at three o' clock on 26 June 1956 was, he tells us, "the only efficient thing we did". Similarly, the narrative foregrounds the gap between Ibbetson's ambitious planning ("the documents were majestic") and the invariably chaotic execution that turned travelling into a "purgatory" for the long-suffering passengers. Instead of the carefully packed provisions and equipment that could be expected from a well-run expedition,

Paton found himself "sleeping on pots, pans, the edges of spades, the rims of iron boxes, and the points of crowbars". He notes that the only one for whom these excruciating travelling conditions was no hardship was Ibbetson himself, since he "had brought a mattress".

From the outset, Paton's narrative also makes it clear that he was less interested in arcane archaeological discoveries than in seeing the sublime Aha Mountains that, in his imagination, "rose, out of a land of rock and sand and stone, unbelievably austere, waterless, plantless, lifeless". This dream-like vision appears to have sustained him during the weeks of arduous travel, and it is perhaps inevitable that the actual experience of finally seeing them could not stand up to the weight of expectation. When the expeditionaries finally reached their long-awaited destination, the moment of dramatic achievement became deflated into anti-climax as the mountains revealed themselves to be nothing grander than "a number of low hills". Even the enigmatic name, "Aha Mountains", so full of allure and promise, turned out to be nothing more than colonial mis-pronunciation, a fabrication that caused the local guide and police constable "to smile". Predictably, this expedition, like the many before it, also failed to find any signs of the fabled Lost City and Paton, to his credit, immediately gave up on the idea. Others in the party were less easily discouraged, however. Jock Flower, for instance, remained convinced that the Bushmen "were lying" when questioned. He afterwards told the *Natal Witness* of his plans to resume the search the following year: "I fully expect to find the city. I am convinced that it does exist despite the many decrying remarks made of Farini's claim. I would like very much to find it because it is there."[35]

Though scouting for the Lost City ruins proved unsuccessful, there were other compensations for Paton. A keen amateur ornithologist, he found much pleasure in the rich and prolific birdlife of the Kalahari. He notes his delight at identifying "24 species unknown to me", which pushed up his tally of Southern African birds to over 400. Harold Pole seems to have been the only one in the party who came to share Paton's passion for birding. The narrative is punctuated with listings of birds seen and records of new sightings, and also includes methodical observations on grasses, shrubs and trees, reflective of Paton's wider naturalist interests. The scientific names of several species were initially left blank in the manuscript, but then identified in the later typescript version, indicating that Paton probably consulted specialist reference works in order to fill in the gaps. Overall, Paton emerges as an accomplished and meticulous observer of the minutiae in the landscape around him. Larger game, such as the numerous antelope encountered is, by contrast, mentioned only in passing, including the large, hungry lion which, according to Brian Pole, once followed the truck for miles (see p. 56).

The close attention Paton gave to the birds and plants of the Kalahari is complemented by his keen interest in the people he encountered. Throughout the narrative, he shows himself to be fascinated by the various inhabitants of the desert, engaging them in conversation, asking probing questions about their lives and taking care to record each person's name, age, appearance and ethnic origin. Paton's meticulousness extends even to matters of pronunciation, such as when we are introduced to the party's "tall Mchuana" guide, R. Harry Mhapha, whose name, Paton takes care to tell us, is "pronounced roughly Em-Harper, the 'r' silent as in British English". For Paton, the people of the Kalahari are clearly not merely a picturesque part of the landscape, but are to be engaged with respect, as individual human beings. Several verbatim conversations are also recorded, most notably with David Frans and Katrina Whiteman at Tsane. A visual record of this latter encounter, in the form of the photograph taken by Spencer, shows Paton and Whiteman sitting in comfortable proximity to each other on the edge of Tsane Pan (see p. 40). On Paton's lap we can discern the diary in which he recorded their conversation. The diary entry of 3 July 1956 includes his interview notes. Like the narrative, the diary reveals Paton's curiosity about the racial identity of his young interlocutors and the apparent anomaly of being "white coloured".

In the context of Paton's sympathetic engagement with the people of the Kalahari, his description of the party's encounter with the Bushmen of Ghanzi tends to strike a somewhat jarring note. Paton writes here that his "first acquaintance with such primitive human life" produced in him "a revulsion", which he ascribes not so much to the Bushmen *per se* as to "their nasty and brutish life". The bluntness of these admissions might well be disturbing to contemporary readers, schooled in a different attitudinal ethos, especially since Paton's condemnatory tone here seems so much at odds with the liberal humanist values that his better-known works espouse. Paton himself was clearly troubled by his own reactions and is at pains to distinguish between the antipathy he feels for the Bushmen's lifestyle and the people themselves. He notes that had he stayed longer with them, "no doubt I would have, like many before me begun to have an affection for them". Paton's negative remarks about the Bushmen should be understood in the context of the conventional attitudes of the times. The Bushmen, in the mid-1950s, were still regarded by many as primitive and not wholly human on account of their "different" appearance and "non-civilised" lifestyle. Paton's references to "tame" and "wild" Bushmen similarly follow the conventional terminology of his day. These distinctions were derived from standard colonial divisions at the time – "tame" Bushmen denoting those who would willingly engage with or actively sought out European company (and were readily inducted into domestic service or labour), while the latter category referred to those who shunned European contact and resisted being brought under the ambit of white "civilising" influence. "Wild" Bushmen were regarded as unpredictable and potentially dangerous, to the extent that when camping in their territory, the nervous party spent a wakeful night, for they had been told stories by their guides of Herero horsemen being murdered in their sleep for their tobacco. After his first encounter with the Bushmen at Ghanzi, Paton's attitudes undergo a discernible shift, and his meeting with the "tame" Bushmen of Xhubi is described from a much more empathetic perspective. He describes them as "sleek and clean", which he attributes to "the nearness of water and the regular food". He is able to engage with them on a more personalised level, and records his encounter with a "pretty young tame Bushwoman, with the wild name of Xhwae Booe", as well as a whimsical exchange, through an interpreter, with one of the Bushmen about his broken spectacles.

It is perhaps inevitable that Paton's depictions of the Kalahari Bushmen will be compared to those of his friend and contemporary, Laurens van der Post, whose landmark text, *Lost World of the Kalahari* (1958), did much to fundamentally shift public opinion around the Bushmen. Paton's and Van der Post's paths must have almost literally crossed in the Kalahari, and their respective journeys took place within a few months of each other.[36] Despite this temporal and spatial proximity, their respective travel narratives reflect very different conceptions of the Bushman people, and it is interesting to compare them. Van der Post's *Lost World of the Kalahari* is a passionate and romanticised homage to the Bushmen, who "moved in the glare and glitter of Africa with a flame-like flicker of gold".[37] His evocative language and Mediterranean imagery create a powerful mythic image of the Bushmen living as pristine First People in an African Eden. They are seen to be possessed of an authenticity and purity of soul that has been lost to modern man. For Van der Post, the allure of the Bushmen lay precisely in that idyll, with its promised recovery of an elemental, more deeply authentic self.

Van der Post's romantic vision of the Bushmen has, however, also attracted criticism for its essentialist tendencies. The Bushmen of *Lost World* are frozen in a stone-age paradigm more in keeping with Van der Post's own nostalgic ideal than the contemporary reality. Nonetheless, his lyrical endorsements of Bushman culture did much to shift public opinion of the time.

Whether Van der Post, whom Paton admired and with whom he was in regular correspondence,[38] played some role in modifying Paton's initial views is open to speculation. What does seem clear is that over the years Paton's attitudes to the "primitive" Bushmen underwent substantial revision. This is evidenced by passages in the first part of his autobiography, *Towards the Mountain* (1980), where he presents a generous and positive assessment of Bushman culture:

> This earthly paradise was lived in by several peoples of whom I shall name two. One were the San people (once called the Bushmen), people of small stature, magnificent hunters and trackers, superb marksmen with the bow and arrow. They knew all about the herbs and plants of the veld, as food, as medicine, and as the sources of some very virulent poisons with which they tipped their arrows. They worshipped the moon and ascribed supernatural or magical properties to certain creatures such as the praying mantis. But their immortal achievement was their rock painting, in which figured humans, animals, birds, and the pleasures of the chase.[39]

One cannot fail to be aware of the dramatic shift in depiction between this passage and the earlier narrative, a shift that in part mirrors the liberalising consciousness and terminology of the 80s, but which is also indicative of the inner journeys that Paton himself had come to make.

Whatever the reasons for its subsequent slide into obscurity, the Natal Kalahari Expedition, and in particular Paton's part in it, remains a fascinating chapter of South African travel history, and it is fortunate indeed that the Lost City manuscript has survived intact. It is a diverting and accomplished piece of writing that shows Paton, the skilled wordsmith, at the height of his literary powers. Although the ambitious venture may have ultimately failed in its stated objectives, it certainly caused a stir in its day. As a result of the extensive press coverage publicising the event, the expeditionaries were inundated by fan-mail. The Ibbetson family scrapbook contains numerous letters from eager young men clamouring to be taken along on the grand adventure.

Paton's last word on the subject of the desert ruins leaves the matter tantalisingly open: "Is this Lost City so sacred to the Bushmen, or the Hereros, or the Batawanas, that no one will breathe a word of its location?" he offers at the conclusion of the manuscript. As for Ibbetsen, he remained convinced to his dying day that the Lost City existed. In fact, the week before he died, according to his son Kevin, he still maintained: "It's there!"

Hermann Wittenberg

NOTES

1. Paton's Lost City narrative as well as related materials are archived in the Alan Paton Centre, Natal Kalahari Expedition, PC 1/7/1/3. Peter Alexander's biography, *Alan Paton. A Biography* (Oxford, 1994), mentions the "harebrained expedition" in passing. Alexander, however, seems not to have read the major narrative text in the Kalahari papers, because he states that Paton "found neither the city nor the Aha mountains" (p. 311). As the narrative makes clear, the expedition did, in fact, reach the mountains and spent four days exploring the area.
2. Paton's second autobiography, *Journey Continued* (Harmondsworth, 1986) deals with the relevant period.
3. The name "Kalahari Polka", mentioned in a *Natal Mercury* article, "'Lost City' Expedition on the way home" (19 July 1956), evidently derived from the truck's lurid paintwork.
4. This quotation and subsequent extracts are taken from Paton, *Lost City of the Kalahari* (see p. 51 of this edition).
5. G.A. Farini, *Through the Kalahari Desert. A Narrative of a Journey with Gun, Camera, and Note-book to Lake N'gami and back* (London, 1886).
6. Kevin Ibbetson, interview with Hermann Wittenberg, 26 May 2004.
7. It is probable that the manuscript was written not long after the expedition ended. Among the Kalahari papers is a covering letter which Jean Ibbetson (wife of Sailor) sent to Paton, dated 20 August 1956. It refers to "rough notes" written by her husband, which were apparently included in her correspondence. There is no record of the notes themselves, but it seems likely that Paton and Ibbetson were collaborating in the effort to produce a written account of the journey. Paton was evidently taking the former part of his duties ("Scribe and Bottlewasher") seriously.
8. The article was entitled "Again the Beloved Country" (21 April 1961), p. 62. Spencer's picture was captioned "Alan Paton (in Bechuanaland)".
9. "'Lost City' expedition", *Natal Witness* (25 June 1956).
10. "'Lost City' expedition", *Natal Witness* (25 June 1956).
11. "To search new area for 'Lost City'", *The Argus* (22 June 1956).
12. Paton, *Journey Continued*, p. 158.
13. "Lost City of the Kalahari", *Sunday Express* (17 June 1956).
14. Kevin Ibbetson, interview with Hermann Wittenberg, 26 May 2004.
15. Brian Pole, interview with Hermann Wittenberg, 23 June 2003.
16. Brian Pole interview.
17. Anonymous diary, untitled, Alan Paton Centre, PC 1/7/1/3.
18. An account of the venture is given in a *Natal Daily News* article, "Five Durban men start new search for £33 000000 treasure" (30 May 1957).
19. "Rand man's first book to be filmed", *The Star* (17 July 1963).
20. Paton's reference here is probably to the film Ibbetson took of the expedition, which has since vanished without trace.
21. All the above quotations are transcribed from the tape recording of the interview which Mark Pole conducted with Alan Paton in 1988.
22. "Natal men fail to find 'lost city' of Kalahari: Returning soon", *Natal Daily News* (18 July 1956).
23. "Natal Expedition to search for 'Lost City'", *Natal Daily News* (29 May 1956).
24. A.J. Clement, *The Kalahari and its Lost City* (Cape Town, 1967).
25. Clement, *The Kalahari and its Lost City*, p. xi.
26. Lawrence Green, *To the River's End* (Cape Town, 1948), p. 28.
27. See for example, "Natal party's search for Kalahari 'lost city' analysed", *Natal Daily News* (2 June 1956).
28. Green, *To the River's End*, p. 34.
29. Lennox van Onselen, *Trekboer* (Cape Town, 1961), pp. 122–123.
30. Clement, *The Kalahari and its Lost City*, p. 25.
31. Clement, *The Kalahari and its Lost City*, p. 25.
32. Fay Goldie, *The Lost City of the Kalahari*, p. 1.
33. Letter addressed to Reg Ibbetson, dated 31 July 1956, kindly made available by Kevin Ibbetson.

34. Herman Charles Bosman, "Lost City", in *The Collected Works of Herman Charles Bosman* (Cape Town, 1988), pp. 181–182.
35. "Kalahari Team Is Still Hopeful", *Natal Mercury* (23 July 1956).
36. Van der Post's Kalahari travels began in September 1954, lasting until the spring of 1955. Paton arrived in the area at the end of June 1956. For a detailed critical account of the context and impact of *Lost World of the Kalahari*, see Edwin Wilmsen's "Primitive Politics in Sanctified Landscapes: The Ethnographic Fictions of Laurens van der Post", *Journal of Southern African Studies*, 21/2 (June 1995), pp. 201–223.
37. Laurens van der Post, *The Lost World of the Kalahari* (London, 1988), p. 10.
38. Paton and Van der Post were friends and corresponded regularly, mostly about Paton's political work, which Van der Post supported through regular and generous donations, but also about each other's writing. However, in none of the letters held by the Alan Paton Centre is there any mention of Paton's Lost City narrative, nor about his Kalahari adventure.
39. Alan Paton, *Towards the Mountain* (Harmondsworth, 1980), p. 47.

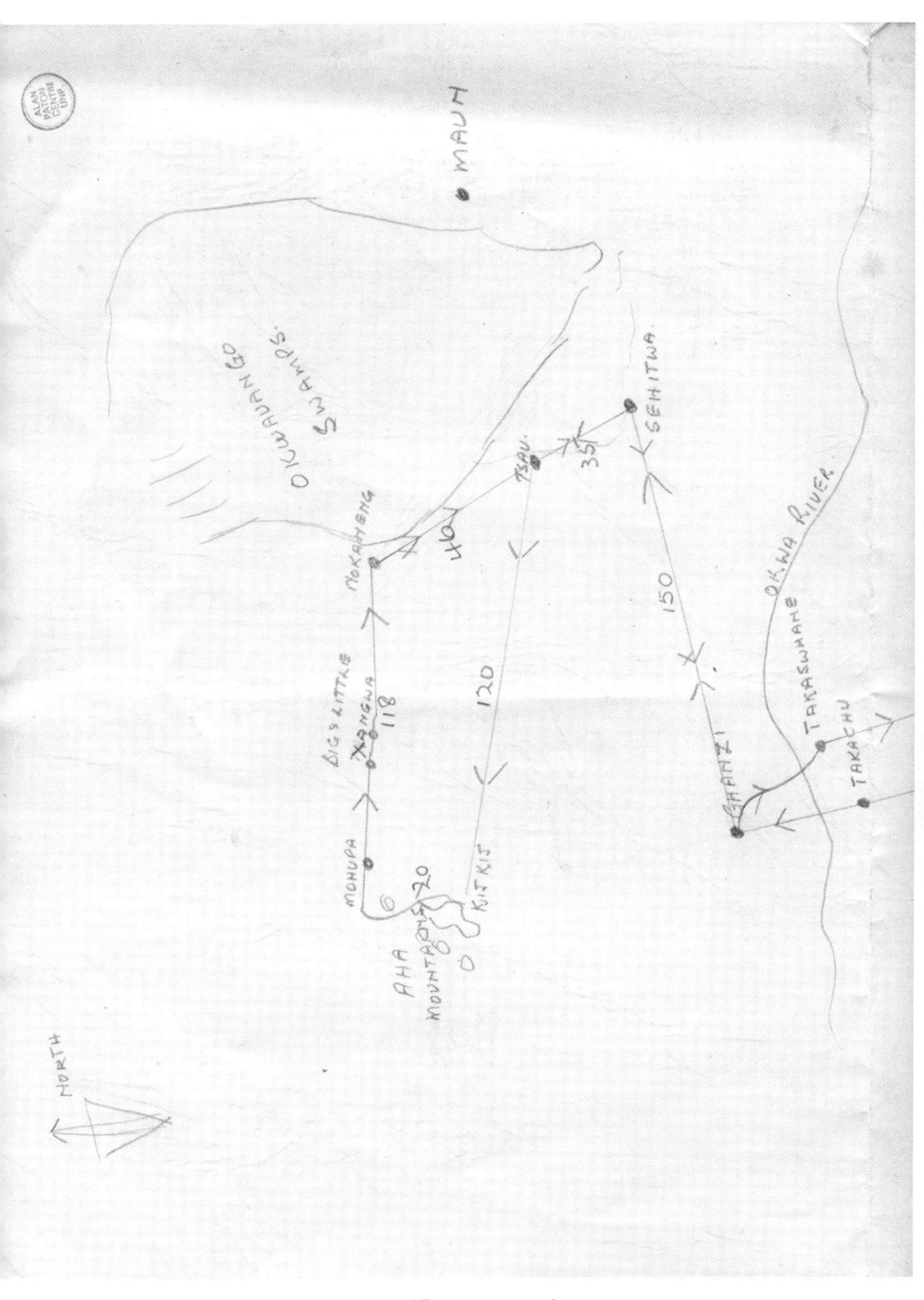

Map showing round route through the Bechuanaland Protectorate to the Aha Mountains, found on a sheet of paper in Paton's diary.

Source: Alan Paton Centre

21A

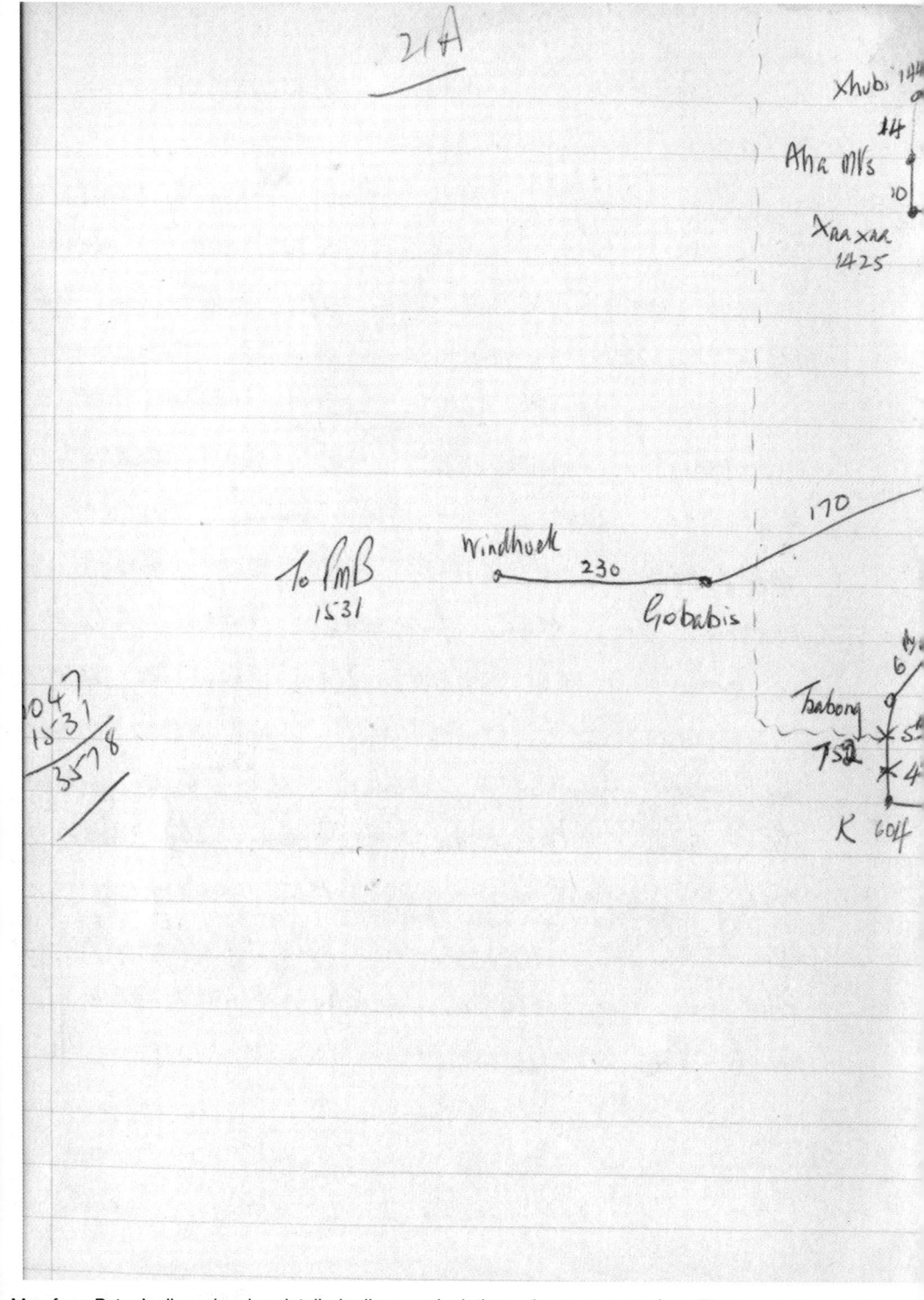

Xhubi 144
Aha m's 14
Xaaxaa 10
1425

To PmB   Windhoek   170
1531   230
                              Gobabis

10 47
15 31   Tsabong
35 78   752

                                          K 604

Map from Paton's diary showing detailed mileage calculations, drawn en route from Pietermaritzburg to the Aha Mountains. The "Xs" probably indicate the various breakdown points. "B.P." stands for Bechuanaland Protectorate.

Xhangwa 1453
Mahupa
100   Nokaneng 1563
's Breasts 46
Tsau 1305-1609
36
Sehitwa 1270
140
7th.
Ghanzi (1120)(1794)
1025
Lehututu   Kang 1955
Tsane   Kukong 2007
920   Khakhea 2042
            Bray 2140

Mafeking 2248

Meyerton 2410

21B

B.P

One night on road.
265
K   3rd night on road   2
444   X
                    Bfn   Winburg
                    389   265

0
2716

Source: Alan Paton Centre

D/C Doc 106.
Mafeking
Map of Dech Pool

75927   Pc1/7

Driving Licence

THE 1956 NATAL KALAHARI EXPEDITION

Arrive Howick as soon as poss., not later than noon

TIME OF DEPARTURE :- 1500 hours from Howick, 26th June, 1956.
Tuesday —

LEADER :- MAJOR D.C. FLOWER.

2 I.C. :- MR. REG. IBERTSON.

1. OBJECT :- To find Lost City, by truck and foot patrols.

   Route :- Howick – Harrismith – Kroonstad – ~~Vryburg~~ – ~~Ghanzi via Tsabong~~
   Kimberley Kuruman

2. EXPEDITION :- To be kept secret. Tshabong –

   EXPEDITIONARY :- Major Flower — Leader & Cook
   Reg. Ibertson — 2ⁿᵈ & Photographer
   Ray White — Driver & Mech
   Keith Walker — Navigator
   Len Tree — Driver & Mech
   Alan Paton — Scribe & Bottlewash
   Brian Pole — Driver & Mech

Revolver –
Belt –
Cash –

A direct Route has been decided on irrespective of what may be found on the way.

Chicken –
Rusks –
Beer for L.T. –
Drambuie –

Mission Document of the Natal Kalahari Expedition, annotated by Paton. A similar copy but with different notes exists in the Ibbetson family scrapbook.

Source: Alan Paton Centre

DUTIES:- (to be decided on at next meeting).

HUNTER	DRIVERS (2 at a time)
GEOLOGIST	LOOKOUT ON TRUCK
PHOTOGRAPHER	SENTRIES
LOG KEEPER -	NAVIGATOR
SCRIBE — ASP.	COOKING
FINANCE SECRETARY	

It has been decied that no one man has the say. (All for one and one for all).

There will be no shooting except by the hunter and his assistant.

Should anything be found a watch party will be left.

Every member must have a yellow fever certificate as nobody can leave the Union without it.

Yellow Fever Certificate:-
If possible to be obtained by the next meeting.
(Can only be done on Tuesday's by appointment).

Everyone must carry side arm with ammunition.

Licences for rifles and small arms to be obtained.

Prospecting licenses.

ADMINISTRATION.

VEHICLE :-   To be supplied on loan by British ~~Diesel's Ltd.~~ *Leyland Albion*

Fuel consumption on a basis of 10 miles to the gallon.

Diesoline required:-   7 - 44 Gallon drums

✓ Truck Insurance for 1½ months.
Engine Oil.
Food
First Aid
Arms and Ammunition
Drinking Water — *1 gal. per head today =*   30
Cable and Winch (Reg Ibertson)
1 - 14 lb hammer
Maps =
Extra Tyres
1 Welding Torch (Ray White)

Estimated Cost :-   £20.0.0. per head
Needed £10.0.0. cash in hand in truck.

FOOT PATROLS:-
Each person

POST OFFICE TELEGRAPHS—POSKANTOOR-TELEGRAAFDIENS.

Class. Klas.	Office of Origin.—Kantoor van herkoms.	Words. Woorde.	Code. Kode.	Service Instructions. Diensaanwysings.	Sent. Oorgesein.
press collect.					

TO AAN natal witness pietermaritzburg

reached ghanzi wednesday 1200 miles from nottingham road and 500 miles into the kalahari averaging six miles per hour leave today for lake ngami after which will come one hundred miles unknown country to aha mountains stop saw remarkable sight of cattle being wattered from wells near tshani pan stop have also seen first bushmen stop arrival ghanzi delayed by accident twenty two hours tuesday truck brought down heavy branch of camelthorn which smashed canopy and came to rest inches from heads of Keith walker and self party well cheerful very dirty paton

Copy of telegraph sent by Paton to the *Natal Witness*. Source: Alan Paton Centre

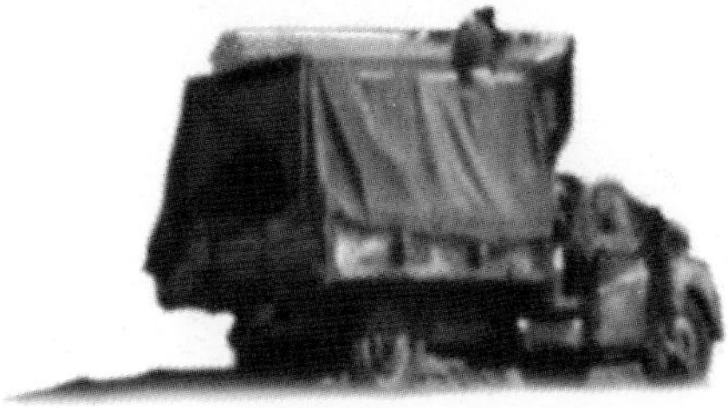

Lost City
of the Kalahari

by

Alan Paton

From left – right (standing): Harold Pole, Alan Paton, Sailor Ibbetson, Major Jock Flower
(crouching): Len Tree, Keith Walker, Brian Pole.

Source: Ibbetson family scrapbook

The Lost City =

1. Picking up Hubber = Tsabong & the Aha Mts. —
2. Setting off from Nothingham — Tsyhr goes up Sat Windburg — Kuruman Half-shaft packs up as we turn N. into the desert ↓ 1st impression] the desert —
3. Crossing the Malopo — We reach Tsabong — Tsane — The great pan — A night trip to Tsane — sand, thorns, plain, forest trees, emptiness, the plain
4. Features of the desert — Grass plains — first trees — bushmen
5. To Ghanzi — The accident — Our first bushmen —
6. To Lake Ngami — Livingstone — The lake — The birds] Tsau —
   To Tsau — Kis life — The Batlalari — Kgosi Moremi] He takes us under Henry Moremi & Maida Gadaire

7. From Tsau — Meadow camp — Fragrant herb camp — First night] Aha Mts — the Shai ↓ First camp at Aha.

8. Exploration starts — A desolate country — The frightened birds — The many "walls" — The frightened "walls" — The pan at Mohopa — Return to Aha Mts — The grand sortie — Wild bushmen —

9. The return — Disappointment — The hill shaft — The hunted elf country — "Very far" — No hunting —

10. The Spell] the desert —

I picked up Sailor Ibbetson on the main road from Pietermaritzburg to Kloof. He was a nice-looking young fellow with clear blue eyes, ruddy face, and a powerful body, though he was little above medium height. I do not know how he came to mention the Kalahari, but it was clear at once that he was a fanatic.

"It's the dream of my life to go there," he said, "and to find Farini's Lost City."

"Farini?" I said. "Who's Farini?"

In 1884 Mr G.A. Farini, an American cattle-rancher, was visiting Coney Island when he made the acquaintance of Gert, a half-breed hunter from South Africa. Gert had gone to New York as an interpreter for a party of "Earthmen", small people from the Kalahari. Gert's account of the Kalahari, its grass-covered plains, its teeming game, and its diamonds, determined Farini to visit this paradise that he had always thought to be a desert. He spent several months there with his son Lulu, observing people, plants and animals, and making notes for his very readable book "Through the Kalahari Desert."

Near the end of his journey he camped beside "a long line of stone which looked like the Chinese Wall after an earthquake." But it turned out to be a man-made wall, built out of worked stones. Farini and his son spent two days there, excavating pavements, and convincing themselves that here indeed had once been "a city, or a place of worship, or the burial-ground of a great nation, perhaps thousands of years ago."

"Haven't other people tried to find this Lost City?" I said.

"They went to the wrong place," said Sailor. "They looked too far to the south."

"Where are you going to look?"

He looked at me out of his blue eyes, and uttered the magic name.

"The Aha Mountains," he said.

"Why them?"

"I flew over them once," he said, "from Windhoek to Maun, and down below me I saw a clearing, and in the clearing a series of parallel walls, and I said to myself, that's the Lost City."

But that was not his only reason. Farini had no compass, no sextant, no mathematics; therefore no one could rely on his observations. Farini wrote of the place Ki-ki, but did I know there was another Ki-ki near the Aha Mountains? Farini went to Lake Ngami, didn't he, and wasn't it possible that he went further north and west, and when the rice gave out, turned south into the Aha Mountains?

The Aha Mountains!

"Will you take me on your expedition?" I said.

"It's done," he said. "You'll never be sorry. We can't fail. We'll find the Lost City."

"I don't care about the Lost City," I said to myself. "I want to see the Kalahari and the Aha Mountains."

Aloud I said, "Who's going with you?"

"My boyhood friend," he said simply. "Len Tree. A rough fellow, very rough indeed, ginger-headed, but true as steel. A first-class mechanic. And I have another fellow who gave me a lift, a schoolmaster, Keith Walker. He'll be our navigator. We don't want to be like Farini. We want to know where we are."

"That's four of us," I said.

"I'll get three more," he said.

He looked at me innocently.

"When I tell people about the Kalahari," he said, "they all want to come."

I set him down at the Hammarsdale turn-off.

"You'll have to organise things well," I said. "You can't play the fool with the Kalahari."

"Everything will be organised," he said, "down to the last spanner and the last bite of food."

He watched me go off out of his calm fanatical eyes. And I myself forgot him and went off to America, to the Fiftieth Anniversary of Kent School, Connecticut.

Meanwhile Len Tree, the rough fellow, added two expeditionaries to the list. One was Brian Pole, another ginger-head, a young lad of 22, a mechanic like Len himself, all agog to see the Kalahari. The other was Major Jock Flower, farmer of Nottingham Road, veteran of both World Wars, a Scot by birth, and a South African by adoption. It was a natural choice that he should be the leader of the expedition. Then Sailor Ibbetson invited Raymond White, a garage proprietor, to be our hunter; the list was complete.

When I came back from America, it was to find that the expedition was on. The expeditionaries had met, and had planned down to the last spanner and the last bite of food. We were to have heat tablets for the fierce days and balaclavas for the bitter nights, tobacco for the wild men and revolvers for the wild beasts; a rifle to shoot for the pot. There were to be fires every night, and every man would have his turn on guard. We were to travel in a new 7-ton truck, which Sailor was to get from a British firm anxious to advertise their product. Nothing less than a 7-tonne would do it, would carry, besides ourselves and our goods, a jeep; and in this jeep we would reconnoitre every strategic yard of the Aha Mountains. We were to carry spare half-shafts, spare tires, spare crownwheel, three 44-gallon drums of water, six 44-gallon drums of gasoline, a spare gearbox, a spare engine. Raymond White, our newest recruit, was to bring the jeep and be the hunter. We were to take cameras and cine-cameras. We were to bring back a record of a search whose results would shake the world.

These preparations impressed me. Although I attended only the final one of the meetings, the documents were majestic. The emphasis was on the need for superhuman fitness, iron resolve, loyal obedience. I began to question my adequacy. Although in my youth I had been able to walk 50 miles in a day, that had been 30 years ago. Now my hair was getting white, my feet were not so sure, and it set my teeth on edge if there was sand in my food.

But my excitement carried the day. I had in my mind a picture of the Aha Mountains as clear as if I had seen it with my eyes. There they rose, out of a land of rock and sand and stone, unbelievably austere, waterless, plantless, lifeless; and I saw their colour as that of yellow ochre darkened by umber, because that was the colour of them on the austere and empty map that Sailor spread out on the floor. The truth is we all fell under the spell.

"When do we reach the desert?" I said.

"We leave on Tuesday the 26th of June, at fifteen hours," Sailor said. "We travel all night, and on Wednesday the 27th before dark we are in Tsabong. We're in the Kalahari."

He said the name "Tsabong" as though he were striking a great brazen gong.

"Then at Ghanzi," he said, with that devastating simplicity, "we start the bundu bashing. Right up this parallel, where no wheel has ever been before, straight to the Aha Mountains."

"And there," he concluded, fixing me with his smouldering eyes, "we'll find the Lost City."

"Have you got the 7-ton truck?" I asked.

"It's in the bag," he said.

* * *

What happened to the 7-ton truck, I never really discovered. Raymond White, disheartened, resigned from the expedition, and with him went the jeep and the rifle, a few days before we were to set out. I tried to reach Sailor and when I did, he told me he had another truck, a good second-hand 5-tonner, in the bag. I received an anonymous letter warning me against the whole expedition. My wife urged me not to go. Kalahari experts began attacking the entire proposition as a waste of time. "Read Farini's book," they said, "he was hundreds of miles to the south of the Aha Mountains." American and British papers began to take an interest in us. Johannesburg was hourly on the phone, asking me to reply to these expert attacks. "Life" magazine badgered me to take their photographer: I referred them to Jock as leader, and Jock referred them back to me as his cultural and literary aide. I frankly didn't want "Life" to come; the photographer would expect trucks, jeeps, sleeping bunks, cartographers, geologists, and iced Coca-Cola. If I had had courage, I would have resigned too.

But I didn't; Sailor, that Ancient Mariner, had fixed me with his eye.

* * *

We were due to leave Nottingham Road at three p.m. We left on the minute. This was the only efficient thing we did. I, aging man, found myself lying on a mess of pots and pans, in the body of an ancient truck, over which an ancient canopy had been erected. The wind roared through it, sending it bellying in, then plucking it madly out, then suddenly, flicking a corner of it wickedly at one's eyes. I bumped about breathlessly, with two great anxieties in my mind: One, could I stand it? Two, could the "Life" photographer stand it too?

In spite of my worries I examined Len Tree curiously, the rough fellow as true as steel. He was a small ginger-headed man with a tremendous moustache and a woollen night-cap with a pom-pom top, meant to be worn privately. He lay down on an iron box, and reaching out one arm to grasp a straining strut of the maddened canopy, went to sleep.

In the front, in the driver's cab, his fanatic friend sang as though his heart would burst. Behind us came the cars of the newspaper boys. They looked incredulous and supercilious, but a trained observer could see envy too.

* * *

We did not reach Tsabong the next day, nor the next nor the next nor the next. When we were due at Tsabong, we were still camping on the high plateau of the Orange Free State, during one of the bitterest winter spells for many years. We had done only 200 miles when the truck came to a grinding stop. I began to wish I had taken my wife's advice. But if I had I should have missed acquaintance with two of the world's most irrepressible mechanics. They made a shear-legs out of planks, lifted the engine out, and found the crankshaft broken; so we hitch-hiked into Bloemfontein and got a new one. Thirty-six hours later we resumed.

Meanwhile Terry Spencer, the "Life" photographer, had arrived. He was one of us in a very short time. He was made assistant dishwasher to me, and never once did I get the impression that he really liked the job.

Terry formed a low opinion of the truck. If this is what happened on the national highway, what would happen in the desert? Our leader Jock must have had the same thought too. He looked burdened with care.

* * *

On Thursday the 28th of June at six p.m. the Natal Kalahari Expedition resumed its way. We passed through Bloemfontein and Kimberley in the night, and left Barkley West into the bitter dawn. We had left the grass country, and were in an arid world of rock and thorn. We had the unmistakable feeling that one gets when civilization comes to an end, the excitement of the unknown. Why, of all the people that I knew back home, not one had ever made this journey. We reached Kuruman, the last town of the Union of South Africa.

"You needn't go any further," we were told by John Cowburn, owner of the Kalahari Pharmacy, "Kuruman is the Lost City."

He and others loaded us with kindness and gifts, and with professional eye, condemned our truck.

"It'll never do," they said. "Two small trucks, yes. But a 5-tonner will never get through the sand."

It seemed a pity to leave Kuruman in the dark on this first step into the unknown. But we didn't go far. The front right wheel developed an ominous knock, and at midnight we pulled out our sleeping bags and camped out at the side of the road.

It was Friday the 29th when we finally turned north towards Tsabong, one hundred miles away; although still in the Union of South

From left: Major Flower, Alan Paton and Sailor Ibbetson   *Source: Ibbetson family scrapbook*

Africa, we were now in the Kalahari. The road deteriorated at once and became two tracks in the sand. Our speed dropped to six miles an hour; we ground along in auxiliary low gear, with the gearbox screaming.
 It was a sound we were going to hear much of for the next 1 500 miles. We were hardly in the Kalahari before the truck stuck in the sand; we all jumped out, shovelled away the sand from the wheels, and laid down the steel mats; with a jerk and a groan the truck moved on again. Calamity came soon after; we saw approaching us from the other end of this rudimentary road another truck, and Brian Pole politely moved off the tracks. Our truck wavered, then stopped. Brian reversed immediately, and our wheels dug in.

The driver of the other truck, Farmer de Klerk, drove nonchalantly into the grass and halted. He gave us no false comfort about our truck; it was too big and heavy for such sandy roads. He also advised us to let the other fellow be polite; the other fellow knew how to drive in the Kalahari and we did not. He waved us goodbye, and drove nonchalantly out of the grass onto the road. We were left a bit subdued by this criticism of our truck, and that, before we had even entered the Bechuanaland Protectorate. So Brian let out the clutch with a defiant roar, and the battle between truck and sand was on. Defeat was instantaneous; the left half-shaft broke just outside the spline.

There were no hard words; within a minute Sailor and Brian and Len were getting out the tools. Jock kept up our spirits by saying that such things must happen. Terry and I went for a walk. We both agreed that the chances of seeing the Aha Mountains were remote; we condemned utterly the schoolboyish slap-dash of the whole expedition. We returned to find that many of the teeth of the crownwheel were cracked, but the spare could not be put in because the bearings were the wrong size. True, we had another spare half-shaft, but we knew we would have to travel 1 500 miles through the sand. The prospect was gloomy.

Yet one could not stay gloomy. There were Len and Brian whistling at their work, Jock and Keith poring over the map, Sailor and Harold Pole preparing a fragrant stew, Terry photographing right and left. After a good meal our mechanics finished the job, and we spread out on sleeping-bags in the middle of the road and went to sleep. No one kept a fire going, and no one mounted guard. It was the craziest expedition that ever entered the unknown.

* * *

The Kalahari is not a desert of dunes. Although we were to strike sand of every colour and consistency, we saw perhaps two dunes on our entire journey. There are districts where dunes are common, but they form only a fraction of the whole. The Kalahari is a flat desert of trees and grass, the overwhelming majority of the trees being acacias, notably acacia giraffae, the camelthorn and most of the grass being aristida brevifolia, Bushman grass. This kind of country is called acacia savannah, and though it varied from place to place, and sometimes from mile to mile, the elements of the pattern never changed. Sometimes the scene was intensely beautiful, sometimes harsh and desolate. The grass was overwhelmingly yellow, but sometimes there were patches, even fields, of red. Sometimes the grass was short, sometimes so long that the desert looked like a prairie of ripened wheat. But when one walked into it, one saw that the hummocks were widely spaced, and in between them was the everlasting sand.

There are only three rare exceptions to this pattern of plain, tree, and grass. The first is when the acacias give way to, or are interspersed with, the mutsiara, the manato, the maroela, the mukwa, and most exciting of all, the great baobab or cream of tartar tree. The second exception is when an eminence rises out of the desert, and this happened to us not more than three times, causing always a pleasurable excitement. The last exception to the monotony is the pans, flat and roughly elliptical open spaces, filled with shallow water during the rains, but now dry, with a white chalky surface made rough by the hooves of antelopes and sometimes cattle. Some of these pans are thousands of acres in extent, strange and majestic, surrounded by low hills; others are not bigger than a good-sized room.

The mean altitude of this desert is over 3 000 feet and it enjoys an average rainfall of ten to twelve inches. The day shade temperature on our mid-winter journey frequently reached the 90s, and the night temperature was often near freezing, and once, below it. Its population is a few thousands, but that of the whole Bechuanaland Protectorate is over 300 000. The Kalahari is a land of fugitives, for here the Bushmen found sanctuary from the Boers and the African tribesmen, the Hereros found sanctuary from the Germans of South-West Africa, the Bakalahadi fled from the Bechuana, and the Matabele from the Zulu tyrant Shaka. Here also are to be found the Hottentots, and Cape Coloureds from the south, and mixtures of all the races, two by two.

Is it a true desert? It is nothing like as harsh and bare as the Great

Karoo of South Africa, and bears no resemblance to the Sahara. If it had water, or if its sand would hold water better, it would be a wonderful cattle country. As it is, the pans are its nodes of life, 10, 20, 30, or 50 miles apart. Here cattle and humans can live, together with millions of flies.

At one time the Kalahari teemed with game, but now antelopes are to be seen in large numbers only in protected areas. Here we saw great herds of springbok and wildebeeste, sometimes 500 or 600 together. The springbok is a national emblem of South Africa, a graceful antelope with an incredible spring which gives it its name. We also saw numbers of gemsbok, hartebeest, kudu, duiker, and occasionally the small delicate steenbok. We saw only one lion, and that on a night journey; porcupines were common at night; and in the heat of the day we ran over an adder, four feet long, and with a girth of twelve inches at the middle – an ugly repellant deadly creature, with not even a sinuous beauty.

The Kalahari is surprisingly rich in bird life. I had no real opportunity to study it, because I always felt unable just to wander off into the bush while the others were servicing the truck, making fires, and preparing meals. I saw a hundred species in odd moments, but I could possibly have reached 200 with more time; nevertheless I was delighted to identify 24 species unknown to me, and to bring my South African total to over 400.

We would travel mile after mile and see hardly a bird; then suddenly they would begin rising from every bush and tree. My only satisfactory pupil was Harold Pole, who began to identify the commoner birds with ease. Our younger members called him Pops, just as they called me Uncle. Pops had proved himself to be the most unselfish of our company, and even brought coffee to our sleeping bags at rising time. He was a long gangling fellow, ginger like his son, and he wore a fantastic green wide-awake hat, anchored under his chin by a piece of string.

I was myself a strange sight by this time. My beard was extremely ugly, brown and grey but with no real flow to it. Sailor's beard was truly magnificent, and no one could have looked more like Henry the Eighth in his most dissolute moments. Sailor's beard was like the waving yellow grass of the Kalahari, while mine looked more like its unkempt scrub. The hair on my head was bleached a sort of dirty white, and whether because of this or for some other reason, I was treated throughout with an unfailing, but unostentatious consideration. Actually Jock was a few years older than I, but he presented from beginning to

Sailor Ibbetson

Source: Ibbetson family scrapbook

end a spick and span appearance, partly because he refused to grow a beard.

* * *

At long last, five days after departure, we crossed the Malopo River, in which no water had flowed for several years. It was real yellow country, with tall waving grass in which we saw our first ostriches. We were now in Bechuanaland, and the track suffered its second sudden deterioration. The temperature in the cab was 100 degrees Fahrenheit, and it would drop that night to 40. This extraordinary range is one of the characteristics of winter in the Kalahari.

We arrived at Tsabong four days behind schedule, and from then on we were to do a great deal of driving both day and night. This was not unpleasant for the drivers, but for the non-drivers it was purgatory. One would start off with the illusion of great comfort, but before long it was clear that one was sleeping on pots, pans, the edges of spades, the rims of iron boxes, and the points of crowbars. This was no hardship to Sailor, who had brought a mattress. Most remarkable of all to me was Brian, who would sleep with his head on one drum, his stern on another, and his feet on the third; these drums had sharp raised edges, but Brian, with the minimum of blankets, would sleep like a log. As for myself, there were times when I wanted to scream out, not through pain, but a kind of muscular agony that, as the hours wore on, became unendurable. I would try to move a foot, but someone would be lying on it, with what seemed to me in those dark hours to be a brutal indifference to my suffering.

Yet there was something compelling about those strange nights. When the track narrowed, the thorn branches would excoriate the canopy from end to end, and it sounded like great waves passing alongside and over a struggling ship. At times the gearbox screamed, at others we reached top gear, which was rare, and hurtled through the Kalahari night at what seemed to be incredible speed.

I do not know how many thorns there are in the Kalahari, but it is clearly of the order of millions of millions. They took their toll on us. Our younger expeditionaries loved in the daytime to sit on the roof of the cab, or on the outside drums, so that they could feast their eyes on this fascinating monotony of plains and grass and tree. It was like a drug of which one could never have enough. But the thorns tore the hats from the heads, the shirts from the backs, the flesh from the bones. Len Tree suffered a nasty wound in his mouth, and Uncle, having visions of an eye left impaled on an angry thorn, retired beneath the canopy. Even there the desert poured in, through the holes in the ancient sail, thorns of camelthorn and red thorn and mutsiara, worms and beetles and stinging wasps and praying mantises of all sizes and colours, sand and dust and seeds from the everlasting grass. These seeds choked the radiator and caused it to boil incessantly, so that we had to protect it with a sheet of fine metal gauze.

* * *

Not even our first pans, which were exciting enough in that Kalahari monotony, had prepared us for the pan at Tsane. The floor is white, and was, I estimated, a mile across and two miles long; though the surrounding sides are not very high, they appear very commanding, and one is tempted to call the whole scene majestic. Over the white floor came hundreds of cattle on their daily trek to the eight wells that are dug in the sides of the pan. These wells must be as primitive as those at which Abraham's servant first saw the beautiful Rebekah. The bucket, weighted with stone, is lowered into the well by men using a rope of cattle hide; when it comes up, boys empty it into a trough scooped out of the trunk of a camelthorn. The cattle stampede and bellow, the boys shout and throw stones at those that want to drink again, the men curse the boys, all this under a cloudless sky and a brilliant light; around us the desert, before us the blinding expanse of the pan. Terry, Harold and Sailor photographed every aspect of the biblical scene; but after a while their subjects grew surly, and wanted payment in advance. There was a nice-looking coloured boy, David Frans, aged eighteen, with unmistakable red in his brown face. We spoke in English.

> Self: What are you, David?
> David: I am a Hotnot.
>
> (David does not know that in South Africa this corruption of "Hottentot" is now a resented word).
>
> Self: How old are you?
> David: (laughing) I don't know. Eighteen perhaps.
> Self: Who is that girl?

David:	Katrina.
Self:	Is she a Hottentot too?
David:	No, she lives in the white village.
Self:	Why does she live there?
David:	(surprised) She is white. She is a white coloured.
Self:	Are you going to stay in Tsane?
David:	(emphatically) No. There is no work here.
Self:	Are both your parents Hottentots?
David:	No. My mother is an Mchuana.

I next talked to Katrina, this time in Afrikaans.

Self:	(cautiously) Katrina, are you a Hottentot?
Katrina:	(emphatically, but quite calm) No, I am a coloured.
Self:	And your parents?
Katrina:	They are coloured also.
Self:	How old are you?
Katrina:	Sixteen.
Self:	Are you at school?
Katrina:	Yes. Standard I.
Self:	Do you live in the white village?
Katrina:	Yes.
Self:	What do they mean by white village?
Katrina:	We are not Hottentots. We are white coloured from the Cape.
Self:	Do you like to stay in Tsane?
Katrina:	Yes. It is nice here.
Self:	What is your full name?
Katrina:	Katrina Whiteman.

But now the men shouted at Katrina. Perhaps she should have been preventing the cattle from coming for a second drink, and not talking to a white stranger.

So we left the great pan of Tsane, called in briefly at the store at Lehututu, and settled down for another night of agony in the truck. Sailor was driving, and he had only one thought in his mind, and that was the Aha Mountains. He urged the truck along through the darkness at what seemed a breakneck speed. One of the struts caught the branch of a giant camelthorn; it crashed down on the canopy, one ton of it, and came to a shuddering rest some three inches from my face. I was saved. When I got down from the truck, I looked for Sailor, but he had hidden away in shame.

Paton at Tsane Pan with Katrina Whiteman.

Photo: Terence Spencer (courtesy of *Gallo Images*)

It was that day that we saw our first Bushmen, not far from Ghanzi. Just how pure the Bushmen of the Kalahari are now, no one quite knows. But these were as small, as dark, as lacking in possessions as any we saw on our journey. One thing was certain, they were not "wild". They had obviously sat waiting by the side of the road; perhaps they had heard us 50 miles away, who knows? They accepted tobacco eagerly, and quite clearly posed for their photographs. Terry Spencer made me throw oranges so that the children could catch them, and it took only a few seconds to get them to enter into the game.

The men were just over five feet in height, the women a little shorter. Some appeared of tremendous age, but perhaps they were not really old, for a nursing mother with babe looked at least 60. The men wore nothing but a girdle, from which ran, from front to back, a black piece of cloth under the crutch, like a pair of swimming trunks almost simplified away. The women wore little more; what clothes they wore, some of skin and some of manufactured cloth, were also black. I never saw a Bushwoman with a coloured cloth in the entire Kalahari; they invariably drew black lines on their faces and these women had drawn one black line along the eyebrow and one above and parallel to it, three short parallel lines at the outer corners of the eyes, and one vertical line between the eyes. Some Bushwomen exhibit steatopygia in small or great degree, that is the accumulation of fat on the buttocks, which is said to be Nature's provision for the unborn child in times of hunger. Neither men nor women are beautiful, their hollow backs, protuberant bellies and spindly legs prevent it.

When no bountiful stranger passes, they live off the land, killing and eating when they can. S.S. Dornan, who has studied the Bushmen, says that two Bushmen will eat a buck at a sitting, and leave nothing but the horns, the hide, and the bones. Thus the stomach is enormously distended, and when it subsides, the skin is disfigured by ugly vertical folds. Everything is food – birds, snakes, all antelopes, lion and zebra, rats and mice, ants and grasshoppers; they also eat many vegetable foods, including the famous tsamma, tasting rather like a withered watermelon, with a high water content that has saved many a Bushman from death.

Of possessions, these Ghanzi Bushmen, except for their bows and arrows, and their pipes and pouches, had nothing. When night falls (and in winter the temperature can drop below freezing), they make a fire and sit round it. They are always on the move, pursuing the game,

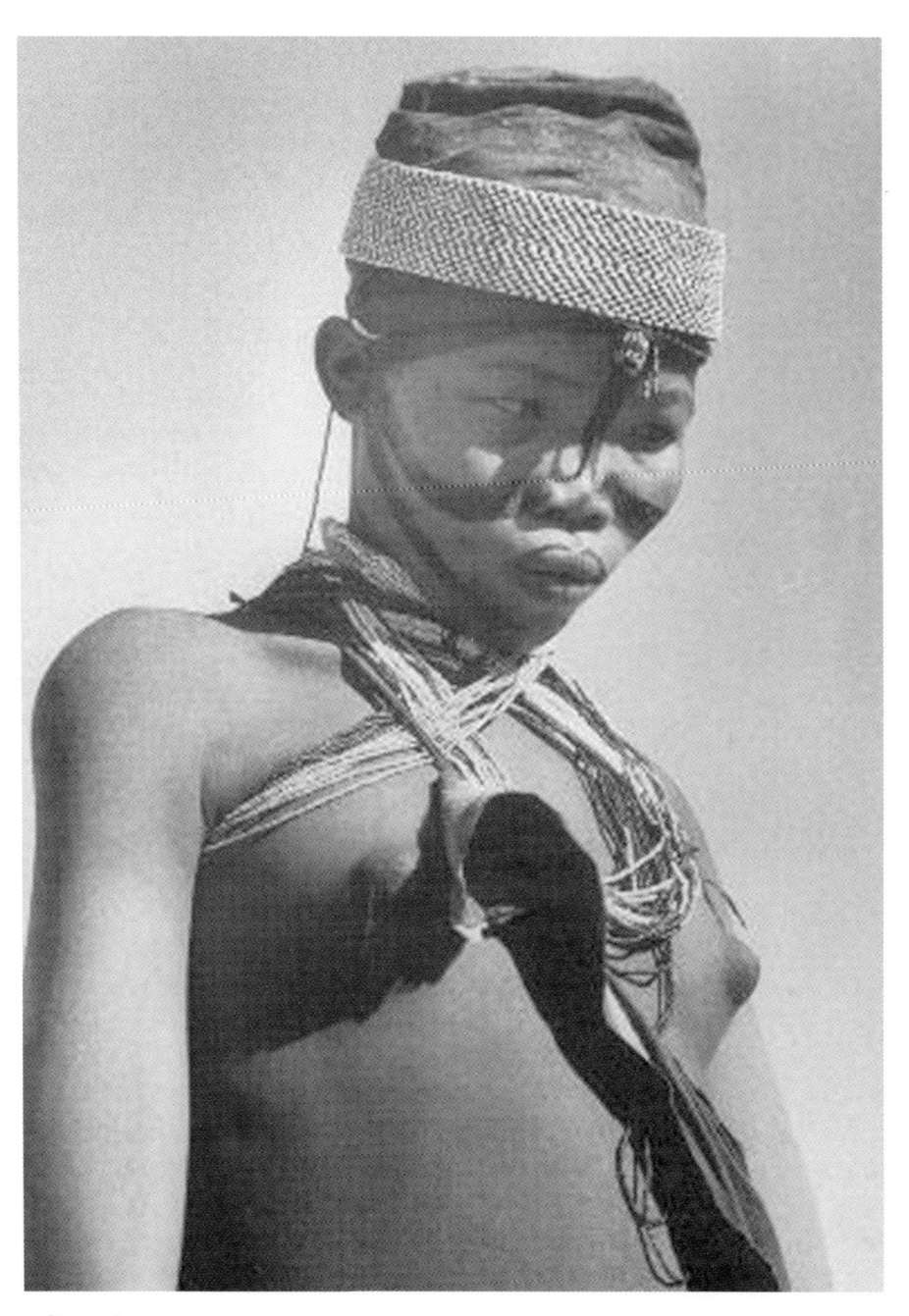

A Ghanzi Bushwoman. *Photo: Terence Spencer (courtesy of Gallo Images)*

but occasionally they build the most primitive of huts, a small tent-like affair as diminutive as they themselves, composed of a few thorn branches, over which is thrown (I would not say woven) grass or leaves. The dust of the arid Kalahari seems to have become one with the skin, even on the head. It was my first acquaintance with such primitive human life, and although it was there before my eyes, I found it hardly credible. Had I stayed with them, no doubt I would, like many before me, have begun to have an affection for them; but as it was I experienced a revulsion, perhaps not so much from them as from their nasty and brutish life, so that I did not really care to stand and observe them. Or it may have been that their skin was dry, dirty, and rough, which is a condition I cannot endure for myself.

While we were with them, they chattered to each other incessantly, in a language in which every word seems to contain one or other "click", explosions of sound caused by the sudden withdrawal of the tongue from teeth and palate. They chatter with abandon, like unselfconscious children; and while they accept gifts with expressions of thanks, they do not pester the stranger for more, as people do in some parts of South Africa. Farini in his book makes mention of this same unassertive behaviour.

At Ghanzi we met still more Bushmen; these were yellow in colour, and presumably had European sires or grandsires. Besides using the black lines on their faces, the women redden their cheeks with what is called "Herero paint". They buy a red powder in the local store called vermilionette, and mix it with oil. The storekeeper told us that, so far as she knew, this powder had no other use; it is made in Holland for the use of Bushwomen in South Africa. These Makoko Bushmen are also far from "wild", and go readily into domestic service with the few white people to be found in and around Ghanzi.

While we were in the shop, yet other short people came in, and we were told that they were Bakalahadi. They are dark in complexion, and Dornan says they are descendants of early Bantu migrants and Bushmen. They speak a primitive kind of Sechuana, the language of the Bechuana people; they too are fugitives, having been driven into the more arid parts of the Kalahari by more vigorous Bantu tribes.

At Ghanzi we learned that Sailor's plan of "bundu bashing" to the Aha Mountains along a parallel of longitude was out of the question. Such a trip would take many weeks and we were advised to go via Lake Ngami, Tsau, and Ki-ki. The Commanding Officer of the Bechuanaland

Police lent us a 303 rifle and gave us ten more rounds; it was foolish, he said, to think we could go without meat. We said goodbye to him and set out on another excruciating night journey, the only compensation for which was the strange and fascinating sound of the waves of thorn, washing over the canopy.

Lake Ngami was a disappointment. It was discovered by David Livingstone in 1851, and Queen Victoria gave him 25 guineas for the deed. It is a dreary place, flat, muddy, and smelly, and the water dirty. Hundreds of cattle are driven to the lake, and the place abounds in flies. The ring doves rise from the roads in thousands. Here we had our first sight of the Herero women; they are tall, sometimes six feet in height, and their height is accentuated both by the built-up headdress which rises some six inches above the scalp, and by the long flowing dresses which reach to the feet. Whether because of this dress or not, they walk in stately fashion, and give the appearance of self-containment.

The Hereros are fugitives also; they were almost exterminated in 1903-05 by the Germans in South-West Africa in one of the most remorseless of settler-native wars, and many fled into the Kalahari, where they are to be found at the water-holes; they are great cattlemen, and some are said to be very wealthy. At Tsau, 36 miles from Lake Ngami, we were met by a great crowd of people, among them many Hereros. There I saw a sweet sight. A Herero man of dignified appearance and about 65 years of age, was standing watching us when he was joined by his wife, a woman of about the same age; her husband, who presumably must have already seen her that day, greeted her with nods and smiles, after which they stood hand in hand and watched us absorbedly. I should like to have had there a couple of my know-all white countrymen, who maintain that married love is a European invention.

We stayed the night at Tsau, in an abandoned house now used by travellers. There we had hot baths, and washed our filthy clothes, after which we had a splendid meal. Tsau was literally alive with birds; the ugly Maribou Stork, doves of various kinds, parrots, ox-peckers, weavers, waxbills, francolins, plovers, louries, rollers, hornbills, drongos, crows – the place was never silent. I saw two birds new to me, the Pearl-spotted Owlet and the Three-streaked Redwing Shrike.

Tsau was to me an exciting place, though whether it would be so to others, I do not know. It is set amongst the usual trees, but is hot and sandy, the frail grass having long since been trodden out by the feet of man and his beasts. Such places are usually depressing, but this was vibrant and alive because of the incessant calling and crying of the birds.

If the desert had been lonely hitherto, now it was to be more so. We were really setting out into the unknown world of Ki-ki and the Aha Mountains. Jock Flower wisely decided to engage a guide, R. Harry Mhapha (pronounced roughly Em-Harper, the "r" silent as in British English), age 58, a tall Mchuana, who could speak Sechuana, German, a Bushman language, a little Afrikaans, and less English. Constable Maika Gaikaiwe, of the Tsau Police, also accompanied us, to enquire about cattle said to have been stolen at Ki-ki. The overburdened truck crawled out unwillingly into the sandy but acacia-wooded roads.

How we would have fared without a guide, I do not know. At times the track was invisible, and one of us would have to run ahead to find it, and even then it was frequently lost. It was said to have been made by Americans, who, said Mhapha, were looking for diamonds; it was now used about once a year by the District Commissioner, and by Herero cattlemen taking their beasts to be sold at Tsau. It must be one of the loneliest trails in all the continent of Africa. We churned along in auxiliary low gear, and slept that night in an utter silence, unbroken even by any calls of the wild. Here we started water rationing, two pints per man, plus five gallons for cooking and washing.

The next day at 8.30 a.m. we entered a wonderful piece of country, a kind of meadow of tall red and yellow grass under the acacias, and out of it rode three African horsemen, who had come 90 miles from Ki-ki and were on their way to Tsau. I thought to myself that they might have been soldiers of Genghis Khan. In South Africa white men would have passed them by, but here we hailed them as fellow-travellers. Sailor astonished me by saying "they remind me of the soldiers of Ghengis Khan." Sailor was in a state of perpetual bliss; when not driving he sat half-naked on the roof of the cab, and feasted his eyes on the monotonous wastes of trees and grass. But his eyes strained always ahead, looking for the Aha Mountains, where the Lost City would be found, beyond the shadow of a shadow of a doubt.

The country here was doubly a waste, unending miles of it having been set on fire. Mhapha said it was the wild Bushmen, who do this to encourage the new grass, which will attract the game. Sometimes we saw their fireplaces, but of them never a sign. We had taken off the canopy, and the truck was inches deep in leaves and insects of many kinds. Some of us were badly lacerated by the thorns; we were filthy and sweaty, and we sat surrounded by bleeding strips of gemsbok meat. But we shouted and sang in a kind of ecstacy born of this desolate waste. Suddenly the trees changed, from acacia to mukwa and manato and mutsiara. The mukwa is a fine timber tree, with splendid naked bole, and bare branches adorned with seed pods of Kalahari beige. The manato is green and well-leaved. The mutsiara is beautiful with red pods and green red-spotted leaves. We were now two days from Tsau, and suddenly on a small rise we were ordered by Sailor to stop.

For there in the distance, barely visible above the trees, were a long flat hill and two lesser eminences. They were the Aha Mountains.

There was great excitement; Sailor was congratulated as though he had made them himself. We all tried to climb on the roof of the cab, which crackled ominously. Photographs were taken, words written, discomforts forgotten. The guide and the constable watched us with amused astonishment. Sailor said to me with emotion, "I'm pent up, I'm pent up." The desert rang with the exclamations of our joy.

The acacias returned and soon after we entered a level open space looking like a golf course, about 200 yards wide. On both sides was the acacia forest, but the open space was covered with short yellow grass, looking like a rough lawn. This was Ki-ki, or Khai-khai according to some, or Tsa-tsa according to Mhapha, or unpronounceably, Xaa-xaa in the Bushmen's tongue. The name Aha Mountains caused both guide and constable to smile; they had never heard of it. Not till we reached home did we learn that some authorities suppose Aha to be the nearest that an English mapmaker could get to the unpronounceable Xaa-xaa. But I hope it will never be changed.

Soon after we came to rest, people came out of the acacias, tall Hereros and short tame Bushmen. The first man we saw appeared to have some skin disease on the face, but we soon saw that he was covered with hundreds of flies. The Hereros appeared to bear this patiently, but the Bushmen kept brushing them away. I was struck again by the ancient appearance of Bushwomen who were suckling their young, and by their ragged clothes and dirty bodies. They clicked and clacked incessantly, rejoiced over the tobacco, made fire with flint and grass, and unlawfully and unseen took one green basin and one bunch of tobacco leaves. Terry, Sailor, and Harold took pictures right and left, while Jock, with the help of guide and constable, made enquiries about the Lost City. It was here at Xaa-xaa that I came to the conclusion that there was no Lost City in these parts. The Bushmen registered total incomprehension; Jock thought they were lying, that they were trying to hide their secret from the white stranger. My own belief was, that had there been a thousand lost cities, we could easily, with the aid of a supply of tobacco and green basins, have found them all.

The flies were so pestilential that we left Xaa-xaa without regrets, and set out on the track to the mountains, which now revealed themselves as a number of low hills about 200 feet above us, set in a rough circle enclosing a portion of the everlasting plain. The trees were manato, mukwa, and mutsiara; and then excitingly, for no climatic reason that one could see, a magnificent baobab, the cream of tartar tree, with its massive trunk that suddenly breaks out into branches, bearing the grey egg-shaped fruits that contain seed encrusted in a white powder which, with water, makes a pleasant acid drink.

The scene was unreal and remote. Though the Aha Mountains had turned out quite other than what I had expected, I was excited to be near them. Indeed we were all excited, and spirits and hopes were high. Jock was clearly relieved that we had reached our destination safely. Sailor was still pent up. And above all, we experienced more intensely than usual the freedom that is felt by the traveller who has temporarily escaped from the world. We debated whether we should mount a guard, this being the land of leopards and wild Bushmen, but we decided against it.

The mountains of Aha are of volcanic origin, and one can often see, in spite of the acacia forest that covers them, low "walls" of outcrop, these very often parallel. Our attention was often attracted by these, and we made several sorties to such places, but none of them was a lost city.

Jock took over the command in real earnest, and organised us into parties, which were to search, as far as that was possible, every part of this lonely country; for it remained Sailor's firm belief that these were the hills under which Farini had seen his man-made wall.

I myself felt that we were too far north, even conceding Farini's unworkmanlike navigation. Nor could I understand why Farini had not described these Aha Mountains which, though in themselves unspectacular, were unique in the Kalahari. But it was really the incomprehension of the Bushmen, and of the Hereros, that convinced me, and I dismissed the idea that they were withholding from us a jealously guarded secret of their gods or ancestors. Nor could I believe that there could be a lost city in a region where the game had obviously been hunted almost to extinction.

A Bushman family group.

Photo: Terence Spencer (courtesy of Gallo Images)

Nevertheless I accompanied the exploring parties, marching through thorny scrub and trees that left their marks on us all. Here we frequently saw the dead fires of the wild Bushmen and the cut stems of reeds that they had taken for arrows. Here we saw, unbelievable in this hot and tinder-dry acacia forest, a flower of wild hibiscus, yellow with a heart of burgundy brown. Most interesting of all to me was the bird-life, far more afraid of man than any I had ever seen in Africa, witness to the presence of meat-hungry Bushmen. Ahead of us we could hear the calls of many birds, but they melted away before us, leaving the whole area deserted and silent. On one occasion I sat down motionless in a small copse for two whole hours before they returned, and was rewarded by seeing, amongst others, no less than six species new to me, the Pied Barbet, Pied Babbler, Yellow-breasted Apalis, Yellow-bellied Eremomela, Tit Babbler, and the Angola Black Tit.

But of Bushmen and of the Lost City we saw not a sign, only the ubiquitous volcanic walls.

At last it was decided to move on a few more miles to Xhubi, a village smaller than Xaa-xaa, and considerably cleaner in respect of flies. We camped on the edge of the pan, a sheet of water about one acre in extent, with longish grass at the edges, set in a stony place surrounded by the everlasting dry and thorny scrub. In no ordinary country could this have been thought a beauty spot, but it was that to us. We washed ourselves and our clothes, and I explored the shores of the reeds, finding Lesser Waterhen, Cape Dabchick, White-backed Duck, Treble-banded Sandplovers, Blacksmith Plovers, Saddle-bill Stork, and other birds. Here we saw a pretty young tame Bushwoman, with the wild name of Xhwae Booe, which means "one loved", with a fine child and a handsome husband, whom I supposed to have some Herero blood, so unlike other Bushmen was he. He made fire for us with sticks, and very reluctantly shot for us an arrow which missed its mark. It was about impossible for me not to conclude that, even in this remote and seldom visited place, he was always on the ready to receive tourists, and to show them the wild life that he himself had, in fact, discarded. Yet this suspicion in no way detracted from the fascination of all that we saw.

The Bushmen of Xhubi were sleek and clean, probably owing to the nearness of water and the regular food. They enter the service of the Hereros as cattlemen, receiving not money but food, tobacco, and security.

After a day's rest at Xhubi, we returned on our track a few miles and camped under a giant baobab, where we built a stockade of thorns; here Brian overhauled the gearbox, while Keith, Harold and I explored the nearby hills. Jock, Terry, Len, and Sailor made a final trip to the eastern slopes of the Aha Mountains. Although the day temperatures were near 100 degrees Fahrenheit, the nights were bitter, and they, without blankets, had to lie almost on top of the fires. On this trip they saw two wild Bushmen; Terry found them by accident while he was searching the countryside through his binoculars. The Bushmen, not knowing they were observed, sat immobile on the rocks, but when the party moved towards them, they vanished without trace. The party spent a wakeful night, for Mhapha and Gaikaiwe had told us that the wild Bushmen were to be feared. In 1954, Gaikaiwe told us, three travelling Herero horsemen had been murdered in their sleep for their tobacco, but their killers had never been found.

Our party returned downcast, having found nothing and knowing that it was time to begin the long journey home. Sailor, usually so exuberant, after one savage outburst, in which he castigated the dead Farini in magnificent and unprintable language, fell into morose silence. But before we left Baobab Camp, I had, through our guide, an unforgettable conversation with a tame Bushman, who held me spellbound because he wore a pair of spectacles with only one lens.

Myself:	Ah, I see you wear spectacles?
Bushman:	That is true.
Myself:	Why do you wear them?
Bushman:	They help a person to see better.
Myself:	Do they help you to see better?
Bushman:	No.
Myself:	Then why not throw them away?
Bushman:	They keep the wind out of my eyes.

We now set out on the lonely journey via Xhabe, Mahupa, and Xhangwa to Nokaneng, after which we would turn south, back to Tsau, and so home. Jock and Sailor, still clinging to the belief that the Lost City was in this part of the Kalahari, now intended to explore a site near Xhabe, where there was said to be a hill, but the rest of us were looking forward to seeing Xhangwa where, we were told by many, the water actually ran. By now it was only with difficulty that we could imagine such a scene, and we set out in good spirits, along a track made dangerous by stretches of sharp-edged volcanic rock. The heat was intense, but we had to run in front of the truck, moving the sharpest rocks off the road. In the late afternoon we saw a tall palm rising above the scrub, and were excited by the unusual scene, having seen nothing like it in the whole desert. We had visions of an oasis, but not another palm did we see. Xhangwa is no oasis, but a series of pools on an expanse of volcanic rock; in order to pass from one pool to another, the water may be said to run, but one must strain one's ears to hear it. We saw no Bushmen here, but some Hereros came to offer leopard and other skins for sale. One of these visitors wore a woman's once-blue coat over a green jersey exposing his midriff, green socks, patched corduroy shorts over patched woman's bloomers, boots tied with grass, and a khaki hat of immense age. When our purchases were made, our visitors showed no intention of leaving us, but sat down and watched us bathing, cooking, and eating. As we were visitors to their country, we could hardly demand that they should leave us, so that night we mounted our one and only guard of the Kalahari journey.

The road from Xhangwa to Nokaneng, which distance we could not measure but which seemed not much less than one hundred miles, was of all our roads the hardest to trace, the loneliest, and the most desolate. It was first made by Mr G.H. Pretorius, the Stock Inspector of Nokaneng, in 1934. The road is used once a year by his successor, less often than that by the police, and occasionally by the Hereros who have cattle to sell, so that it is one of the least-used tracks in all Africa. We had hardly left the last settlement of Little Xhangwa than the right rear wheel sank three feet through an anthill hidden by the grass. Again Brian tried to come out of it boldly, and again the half-shaft broke. All of us knew one thing, that we dared not break another.

The half-shaft mended, we travelled all the following day through hot and desolate country. The effect of fire in this country appeared to be catastrophic, for we passed mile after mile of dead acacia forest, almost without exception old large trees, and underneath them not one sapling of any description. The engine boiled continuously and we had to keep on climbing out to put sticks and leaves under the spinning wheels.

We plagued Mhapha by asking him continually how far it was to Nokaneng, to which he replied "Far, very very far." This particular expression signified something much further than "very far". Even if he said "very far but not so far", that meant ten to twenty miles. The only time he ever permitted himself to mention mileage was when we came within ten miles, when he would say "one mile, and then half a mile", and keep on saying it for at least one hour. Therefore on the third day, when he answered "very far but not so far" we were jubilant, knowing that within a couple of hours we would reach Nokaneng. And so we did, a Batawana village, the most pleasant and cleanest place that we saw in the Kalahari, and having in the person of Mr and Mrs Andrew Wright, a host and hostess full of kindness and Kalahari lore.

* * *

Is there really a Lost City? Did Farini really see it, or did he devote two pages of his truthful and factual book to a piece of pure imagination? Why did his son Lulu, the photographer, take no pictures of the Lost City? Did something go wrong with the camera or the plates? Were the other expeditions right when they went searching in the south-west, in the region of the Auob and Nossop Rivers? Is this Lost City so sacred to the Bushmen, or the Hereros, or the Batawanas, that no one will breathe a word of its location?

I think some of us may go back; not Terry, who liked it once, but would not like it twice, nor Harold nor Brian Pole, for much the same reasons. But the rest of us would go. Not only to search for the Lost City, but also to travel again through the Kalahari. There are strange things to see there, and strange people to meet; but it would be hard to say which is more entrancing, these strange events, or the long passive periods of time that separate them. Certainly the slow passage of time, the absence of ordinary duty, the hot sun burning, the antelopes running, the attractive monotony of the acacia trees and the yellow grass and the everlasting plain, steal over one like a drug. One can never have too much of it, because it is like breathing, something so near to nature that it cannot sate one; one does nothing, one is content to be. And this is true of the nights as of the days, whether one is sleeping under the stars, or lying in agony in a truck, with great waves of sound washing over the canopy.

I have a picture in my mind of Sailor sitting on the roof of the cab, with his great golden beard and his tremendous bare chest, surveying with eyes of bliss the never-changing Kalahari scene, and saying to me out of his strange innocence, "I would spend my life here if I could."

* Images reproduced in the following section have been extracted from original 8 mm film by Harold Pole.

Setting Off

The Truck . . .

The Adventurers . . .

The Route . . .

Camp Life

Catch of the day.

Paton "The Bottlewasher" and Keith Walker.

Brian Pole: Bathroom with a view.

Sailor braaing.

A potjie breakfast.

Keith Walker: Shaving bundu style.

Breaki

Centre: Engine trouble.
Clockwise from right: Boiling radiato
tightening wheel nuts; putting back
trouble.

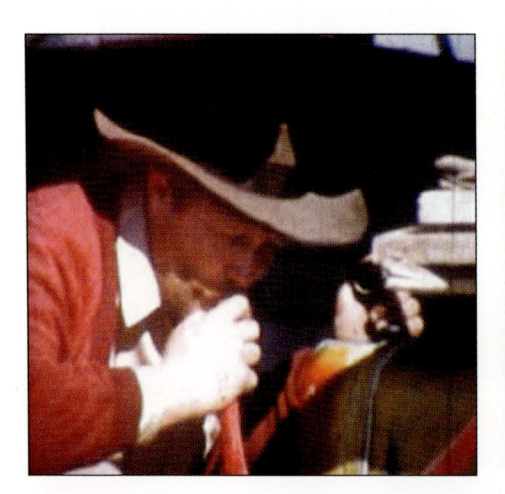

...Down

...out the engine; bogged down in sand;
...e; siphoning petrol; and more engine

Into the Deep Unknown ...

The endless track.

One of the "magnificent baobabs".

A birdwatcher's paradise.

People of the Kalahari

Herder at the well at Tsane Pan.

Bushman demonstrating hunting bow.

Transport by donkey cart: A typical Kalahari scene.

Bundu Bashing

In sight of the Aha Mountains.

Paton looking for the track.

Driving through thorn canopies.

Interview with Brian Pole

HW: First of all, I was wondering how did you – and later your father – become involved in this expedition?

BP: I was working at the garage with Len Tree, who was a big friend of Reg Ibbetson and they wanted a second mechanic, so I said I'd be keen to go. My father, because he was always very keen on that type of thing, also pitched to go and when that chap from Merrivale [Raymond White], who was going to take the jeep, backed out, they said that my father could come.

HW: I'd like to hear more about the truck. It seems to have been in spectacularly bad mechanical condition. How come you landed yourselves with such a vehicle?

BP: Well, Reg Ibbetson had arranged for a truck from Leyland. They said they would lend him a truck. It was supposed to be a big double-axle Leyland Hippo, which would have been completely unsuitable for that trip. When we got to pick it up in Durban, the sales manager looked around for this truck and eventually he found that it had been sold. The only one they said they could lend us was this petrol six-cylinder Austin, which was in a terrible condition. I drove it to Nottingham Road from Durban and it had a knock in the motor, the gearbox was jumping out of gear and there were all sorts of things.

HW: Weren't you very worried?

BP: We were very worried. And we had such limited time to repair this thing, that we just did the very basics. When you think in hindsight now, to go on a trip like that with the vehicle not completely roadworthy was very silly. But we got through, eventually.

HW: In the colour film, which your father made, one can see bright and colourful paintwork on the truck. It looked like a wonderful vehicle, very strange, almost psychedelic. Whose idea was that?

BP: I can't remember. I know I painted the truck but I think we just took paint that we had, mixed it up together and just sprayed. But I'm not really sure why we painted it that colour and whose idea it was.

HW: About the film, the footage that I've seen is wonderful. Where did your father learn this?

BP: He was an amateur, but the family used to go on a lot of trips, to the mountains in Easter time and down the coast. He was very keen on photography. He had this camera and he used to take movies wherever he went.

HW: In Paton's story he comments on the disorganisation of the expedition. There's a press report about the expedition's supply of flour, and also your father's medical kitbag, falling off the truck, just an hour out of Pietermaritzburg.

BP: I think the basic thing comes back to the fact that the truck was in such a bad condition that we spent all the time getting it going. We were determined to go on the date that we had planned. We had wanted to make boxes with lids and bolt them on the chassis to stow things, but we got the truck really at the last minute, so we piled all the things in the back and we said "Right, we'll organise it on the way".

HW: Did all the problems and the breakdowns affect morale?

BP: I don't think so. It seemed to worry Major Flower an awful lot. I think for myself, I was probably too young to worry. But he was terribly concerned. But generally there was quite a bit of friction later on, which I think was partly the fault of the breakdowns. I think partly due to my age they didn't take kindly to my suggestions. Reg [Ibbetson] and I had quite a fight up in the mountains there. We had limited time to look around and they were very determined that we all stick together so that no one got lost. But I said we've got two guides, why not split the party into two lots with two guides and there was a big row about this. It shouldn't have been – why should there be a row about a suggestion like that? And eventually they did that anyway. But that was a minor thing. Generally there was no problem, really. And one of the big things was, of course, that Alan Paton kept everyone going. He never stopped with jokes and talking.

HW: Tell us more about Alan Paton. How did he fit in to such a group? He was a major intellectual and political figure, a world-famous author and one could imagine that there might be difficulties in getting on.

BP: This surprised me, because I felt the same way about him initially, but he fitted in remarkably easily. He was such a gentleman but he got stuck in and helped. Wherever we went in that truck he had jokes and he was talking. He fitted in completely, no problem at all. One night we had a big bonfire and a bit of whisky went flowing and he had a little bit more than he could handle. But he was very embarrassed about it the next day. He was quite a remarkable man.

HW: You mentioned some stories Paton told.

BP: He made up jokes all the time and I can't really remember all of them. But one particular one was where this guide had come on board with some giraffe biltong. Long stretches of meat, maybe two metres long. We were eating this biltong with the guide and then Paton casually started talking about some people he knew who had kids and they lived in this place with all these trees. They eventually noticed that the kids' necks started growing longer, and they were getting very interested in the trees, and so on. It was a long, round-about story, but eventually he got down to the fact that they had been eating giraffe meat. They were of course often silly stories, but he really kept things going. You know, he had stories all the time. He made up stories and he told stories. He was always very interested in everything that was going on. But I think he was also pretty concerned about that truck. He didn't think we'd get back. What I remember of him was that he was always more than happy to wash dishes or do anything else. He never shirked or anything like that.

HW: The perfect travelling companion?

BP: Oh absolutely.

HW: You've read his story. What did you think about it? Did it reflect the events of mid-1956 accurately or were there some things that you were surprised to read about?

BP: I read it again the other day. Generally that was as it happened. There was little mention though of all the game that we saw, which to me was a big thing. In those days you could see an awful lot, which you don't get today.

HW: Tell us more about the wildlife.

BP: I can't even remember the names of all the buck, but on several occasions we would come on a track through the scrub to a pan, teeming with all sorts of buck. These pans were big. The only lion we saw was one day after the canopy got knocked off. So we had an open truck and this lion followed us for maybe two hours during the day. He must have been hungry. It just ran after the truck. Unfortunately my father was driving and he had his camera there in the cab.

HW: I don't know if you were aware of the fact that Paton had earlier that year been elected chairman of the non-racial and anti-apartheid Liberal Party. Did he ever talk about his politics while he was with you on the trip, or was it something he tried to stay clear of?

BP: He made it quite clear at all times that he was not a racist but he didn't, at least from what I remember, talk about politics. He always made it clear that he was pro, but I don't recall him talking about it a lot. There were certainly no arguments that I can remember. In those days it was so very different to now. We were brought up to be anti, and of course at that time he was very much on the other side. I recall Alan Paton at the end of the trip saying to us that we were welcome to visit him at his house anytime – his house was at Kloof, I think – but on condition that we would not be unhappy with whoever was there.

HW: After coming back, did you ever get together again as a party, perhaps for an anniversary?

BP: No, I never saw any of those people ever again other than Reg, but that wasn't on account of the trip. His girlfriend's brother, Lofty Parrot, worked with me and occasionally I saw Reg. But I never saw those guys again, including Alan Paton. I can remember a lot of that trip, but I would have liked to have made notes and taken a camera. I'm sorry that we did not get more pictures of Terry's because he had two cameras. Every single thing he took was with both cameras. He said that if it's something important and there's a problem with that spool at least he's got a backup on the other one. And he took so many pictures.

HW: Do you have any idea why Paton's story and Terry's photos were not published by *Life* magazine?

BP: I don't know, but I presumed it's because we never found anything. And when you think about it, to go there with limited time – we only had a few days up there – it would be impossible. You go out with a guide and you walk and you walk and what are you going to see? It's just such a big area. If the theory was that things would be covered by sand, how could we just walk around and think we'd see a city that's buried in sand over lots of years? Just because it was Reg's idea that it was there. It could have been miles away. We couldn't just dig and expect to find anything. My sister's friend's father lives up there and he reckons he's seen this Lost City, but he can't tell anyone because he's promised the Bushmen. It's just a story, obviously.

HW: But there was some digging done?

BP: A little bit because there was a lot of stone that looked almost like a wall, you could say. It was just a rock formation though. And you'd dig and think "Hey I'm going find something". When I went on this trip I didn't really know a lot about the Lost City and I didn't really think we'd ever find it. So many people had been out to look for it. This expedition was not conducted professionally at all. Reg Ibbetson was a peculiar guy. You know he could talk anyone into anything. I've never known a guy who could talk like that. I remember that I went with him when we had our breakdown. We hitchhiked to Bloemfontein and went into the big LMC [Leyland Motor Corporation] dealership and he went to the manager's office. We came out with a crankshaft, pistons, bearings, gaskets – all for nothing. Reg just got all that for nothing. If I would have gone in there I wouldn't have been in two minutes and I would have been kicked out. But Reg came out with a brand new crankshaft, which costs a lot of money, plus all the other bits and pieces!

HW: He was, I think, at that point a medical insurance salesman? He must have done well.

BP: He was a salesman like you can't believe. Maybe I shouldn't say this but he wasn't always terribly honest.

HW: Do you know about his book, "Kalahari Fever", which was made into a film script, although the film was never made?

BP: What I heard at the time was that there was something they wanted to change in the book. I think it was some racialistic thing. And he didn't want to change it and refused, from what I heard. They said they would publish the book and he would make a lot of money and they would film it, but he would not agree to the changes. When I met him he was actually selling tyres, he was not a medical rep, because he used to call at the garage I worked at. Reg used to come there in the morning when everyone had big overcoats on and Reg would be in a short-sleeved shirt and shorts.

He wouldn't feel the cold. He evidently went on these merchant ships to Russia during the war, and said after that he couldn't feel the cold.

HW: A very interesting man.

BP: Oh, absolutely. But you couldn't help liking the guy. Everyone got on well with Reg.

HW: Looking back, what memories stand out for you from the trip?

BP: You wake up in the morning and your whole sleeping bag is covered in frost. To me this was tremendous. You go to sleep and you just see the stars. It is clear and quiet apart from the animals in the distance. And every morning my dad woke up first and made coffee for everyone. That was his self-elected job. At night we would have these massive big bonfires and we'd sit around talking and that, to me – and the game – was the best of the trip, not looking for a lost city.

HW: And that seemed to be the most important thing for Paton as well?

BP: I'm sure. I can't talk for the others, but Alan Paton and my dad and I didn't expect to find the Lost City, but the trip and the experience of the trip was the big thing. Seeing Bushmen and wildlife, sleeping out under the stars – that to me was unforgettable.

Pietermaritzburg, June 2003

Brian Pole   *Photo: Hermann Wittenberg*

Biographical Note on Alan Paton

Alan Paton was born in Pietermaritzburg in 1903, in the then British colony of Natal. After his schooling at Pietermaritzburg College he attended Natal University College, a precursor to the present University of KwaZulu-Natal. Paton graduated with a B.Sc degree in Mathematics and Physics and subsequently became a school teacher in Ixopo. It is here that he met his first wife Dorrie, whom he married in 1928. In 1935, Paton was appointed principal of the Diepkloof reformatory near Johannesburg. Under Paton's progressive and energetic leadership, the institution, formerly run as a prison for African juvenile offenders, became transformed into a school. Paton's experiences at Diepkloof exposed him to the deleterious social consequences of South Africa's racial policies and shaped his increasingly critical political stance.

In 1946, on an extended study tour of European and American prisons, Paton wrote *Cry, the Beloved Country*, the novel that would bring him world-wide fame. The enduring success of the novel also secured him financial independence, and Paton resigned from Diepkloof in 1948, the same year that brought the National Party to power. In the years that followed, Paton became increasingly involved in opposing the Nationalist's apartheid policies, culminating in his election as chairman of the non-racial Liberal Party in 1956. Paton led the Liberal Party for more than a decade until its forced disbandment, all the while enduring continual security police harassment and the confiscation of his passport. His liberal political outlook and critique of racial segregation policies continued to be articulated through his speeches and writing.

In addition to his well-known novel and a large volume of articles that commented on South Africa's social and political problems, Paton also wrote the novel *Too Late the Phalarope*; biographies on Jan Hofmeyr and Geoffrey Clayton; *Tales from a Troubled Land*, a volume of short stories; as well as several plays and poetry. Before his death in 1988 at the age of 85, he had completed two volumes of his autobiography, *Towards the Mountain* and *Journey Continued*. Paton received numerous international awards, including honorary degrees from Yale and Harvard universities, and South Africa's premier literary prize is named in his honour. He continues to be one of South Africa's most widely read writers.

LOST CITY
KALAH

IS there a Lost City in the Kalahari? Van Zyl, Paver, Lawrence Green, Balsan—all went looking for it, but no one found it. Was it invented by G. A. Farini, who described its ruins in his book THROUGH THE KALAHARI DESERT?

Farini's account does not read like invention. It is matter-of-fact, almost casual. Why should his son make sketches of a ruin that his father had invented? He is said to have taken photographs too. What happened to them?

He had no sextant

FARINI had no sextant, no compass, no navigating instrument, only a map given to him by D. D. Pritchard, of Cape Town, who had been to Lake Ngami by order of Cecil Rhodes. It is probable that the position of the Lost City as given by him was very inaccurate.

That at any rate is the view of Mr. Reg Ibbetson, farmer of Hammarsdale, Natal. He has a passion for the Kalahari, and he is the moving spirit behind the Flower Expedition that will leave Howick on June 26, 1956.

But before we talk of the Flower Expedition, let us hear briefly the story of Farini himself.

Fabulous wealth

IN 1884, in far-off New York, Farini, an American rancher, met at Coney Island a mixed-blood Bushman with the name of Gert Louw.

Louw had been taken to America by a showman, who apparently thought that New Yorkers would pay money to see a man from the desert of the Kalahari. Gert told Farini stories of the fabulous mineral wealth, chiefly diamonds, in his home country.

So in January, 1885, Farini and Gert, accompanied by Farini's son, left New York for this remote desert. The American was an enterprising fellow, and while in London arranged for Gert to be received by the Queen.

Farini, his son, a German trader named Landwehr, Gert and several of his compatriots,

ON Tuesday, June 26, a seven-man expedition, which will include Mr. Alan Paton, author of "Cry the Beloved Country," plans to leave Natal to search for the "lost city of the Kalahari." Ever since the year 1855, when the first news of the "lost

An artist's impression of t...

Reaching a mountain which no one in the party had seen or heard of before, they camped beside a ruined wall, built in a way no Bushman ever knew.

On examination it "proved to be the ruins of quite an extensive structure, in some places buried beneath the sand, but in others fully exposed to view. We

perfect and plainly visible b... neath the layers."

Farini goes on to add a de... criptive piece which as much anything else has convin... readers that he was des... bi... something that he actual... sa... He writes: "The top r... stones were (sic) worn a... v... the weather and the d...